INGRES

INGRES

JON WHITELEY

ORESKO BOOKS LTD·LONDON

(*frontispiece*)
Self-portrait at the Age of Seventy-nine
CAMBRIDGE (MASSACHUSETTS), Fogg Art Museum (Grenville L. Winthrop bequest). 1859. Oil on canvas 65×52 cm. Signed: J. D. Ingres.

By comparison with the *Self-portrait at the Age of Twenty-four*, this portrait, which Ingres painted in 1859 for his second wife, Delphine Ramel, depicts the artist as a proud, successful man of the world, enjoying the honours which came to him after the World Fair of 1855. His coat glitters self-indulgently with decorations. Ingres softened and ennobled his heavy, sagging features, evident in photographs, and his large, drooping mouth was drawn in and posed for the occasion. But his eyes, normally hooded by heavy brows except when excitement would light them up with emotion, have the penetrating acuity of the painter at work. The movement of the composition suggests that the artist was considering an oval format. If so, he must have changed his mind before completion and added the hat to conform to the portrait which he painted for the gallery of self-portraits in Florence the previous year. The two portraits correspond fairly closely although the artist is wearing day clothes in the Florence picture whereas he is in full evening dress in this later version.

ACKNOWLEDGEMENTS

Photographs are reproduced by courtesy of the following, to all of whom sincere thanks are due: Art Institute of Chicago, Chicago; Autun Cathedral; Cailleux Collection, Paris; Ecole des Beaux-Arts, Paris; Fogg Art Museum, Cambridge, Massachusetts; Frick Collection, New York; John Goelet, New York; Hermitage, Leningrad; Baron Robert von Hirsch, Basel; Henry P. McIlhenny, Philadelphia; Metropolitan Museum of Art, New York; Montauban Cathedral; Musée de l'Armée, Paris; Musée des Beaux-Arts, Angers; Musée des Beaux-Arts, Liège; Musée des Beaux-Arts, Lille; Musée des Beaux-Arts, Nantes; Musée des Beaux-Arts, Rouen; Musée du Louvre, Paris; Musée Bonnat, Bayonne; Musée Carnavalet, Paris; Musée Condé, Chantilly; Musée Granet, Aix-en-Provence; Musée Ingres, Montauban; Musée Historique, Versailles; Musée Mandet, Riom; Musée du Petit Palais, Paris; National Gallery of Art, London; National Gallery of Art, Washington, D.C.; Noailles collection, Paris; Palazzo Pitti, Florence; Phillips Collection, Washington, D.C.; Service de Documentation Photographique de la Réunion des Musées Nationaux, Paris; Wadsworth Atheneum, Hartford; Wallace Collection, London; Walters Art Gallery, Baltimore; Photographie Bulloz; Photographie Giraudon; and Novosti Press Agency, London. Plate VI, a detail of which appears on the cover, is copyright the Frick Collection, New York.

Apart from published sources, largely consulted in the marvellous libraries of the Ashmolean and the Department of the History of Art in Oxford, I am greatly indebted for help in one form or another to David Alston, Noelle Brown, Francis Haskell, Robert Oresko, Helen Smailes and, especially, to Linda Whiteley. This book is for Linda and William.

First published in Great Britain by
Oresko Books Ltd., 30 Notting Hill Gate, London W11

ISBN 0 905368 10 X (cloth)
ISBN 0 905368 11 8 (paper)
Copyright © Oresko Books Ltd. 1977

Printed in Great Britain by
Burgess and Son (Abingdon) Ltd., Abingdon, Oxfordshire

Jean-Auguste-Dominique
Ingres

IF A WELL informed visitor to the Paris World Fair in 1855 had been asked to define the essential quality of the paintings exhibited by Ingres he would probably have mentioned their classical detachment. 'His ideal is half good health, half calm, something analogous to the ideal of antiquity' said Baudelaire in his review of the exhibition. Ingres was admired for his mastery of form but no one gave him credit for the imagination, movement, colour and innovation ascribed to Delacroix. And yet Delacroix was the more rational, calculating artist of the two, while Ingres was transparently emotional, isolated from his contemporaries like the archetypal Romantic by a self-destructive sensitivity and a Faustian ambition to succeed. Even so, he might have been no better than Benjamin Robert Haydon, spilling the passion of a Michelangelo into dull art, had he not mastered the conventions of the academic tradition with an irresistible talent and then, like Delacroix a generation later, broken them unerringly for the sake of self-expression. The early education of Delacroix was probably very similar to that of Ingres, but the radical alternatives available to a restless student in 1800 were not at all like those at hand in 1820, and this difference of age placed a constant barrier between the rival claims of Delacroix and Ingres, especially in the 1850s when, if Delacroix seemed the last survivor of Romanticism, Ingres had achieved the status of a fossil.

Jean-Auguste-Dominique Ingres was born in 1780 in an age which encouraged sensibility. The Gothic novel, which he read with evident approval, was a European cult when he was young and, like Goya and Fuseli, he was attracted by the horror of a nightmare as a subject for a picture. Although he did not, in the event, paint any scenes inspired directly by Gothic novels or by his dreams, the dark, stormy night in *Roger Freeing Angelica* (Plate 39), lit by a flaming beacon on the crags, for which there is no justification in Ariosto's text, belongs to the familiar landscapes of Ann Radcliffe's novels. The new emotionalism of Gluck's *Orpheo*, Mozart's *Don Giovanni* and Beethoven's symphonies moved him with religious awe, and he had a proverbial fondness for the violin, which he took up professionally within two years of Mozart's death. He was pompous, serious, yet unaffected, with a peculiarly French sense of dignity. His father, a jobbing sculptor in Montauban, had trained him from an early age to make his career in art, but Ingres did not follow him to become a provincial craftsman, working at the beck and call of patrons. Between the father and the son the eighteenth century interposed the machinery of academies and art schools, which raised the status of the artist and placed the history painter on a level with a man of letters or a priest. Ingres was destined to become a genius by profession.

At the age of eleven Ingres entered the Académie in Toulouse. By the time he left six years later to finish his studies with David in Paris, he had already acquired the mastery in the art of drawing and painting from the nude model which was basic to the academic programme and which always remained the starting point in the preparation of all his paintings. He had also acquired his passion for the art of Raphael, inspired by a copy of the *Madonna della Sedia* (fig. 1) in his master's studio in Toulouse and he returned obsessively throughout his life to this image of tender motherhood, fusing the Virgin's features with the Venuses and odalisques of his imagination and inserting her, like a leitmotif, into a number of his early works.

Ingres rapidly mastered the conventions of contemporary Classicism; the transparent glazing and scumbling of his studies (Plate 2) and the thin, fluent paint of several of his portraits (Plate 7) recall the influence of David. He rose with ease through the hierarchy of competitions at the Ecole des Beaux-Arts, eventually winning the coveted Prix de Rome in 1801, which allowed the successful candidate to spend four years studying in Rome at the Ecole de Rome. Had Ingres left Paris in 1801, he might have had a conventionally brilliant career, but the government delayed his departure for reasons of economy until 1806, giving him instead a small salary and a studio in the disused convent of the Capuchins, where he was in contact with the most lively elements in David's studio. The overblown intensity of Girodet, who worked in a neighbouring cell in the convent, clearly impressed the young Ingres and a number of contemporaries looking for a radical alternative to the teaching of David. The puffed out type of beauty, characteristic of Ingres's women, with their swelling throats and Grecian profiles, was originally derived by Girodet from the conventions of Greek red figure vase painting (Plate 29). This influence was complemented by Ingres's respect for François Gérard,

fig. I RAPHAEL
Madonna della Sedia
Florence, Palazzo Pitti

Dated by Fischel to 1514/15, this tender,
richly coloured image of the seated Madonna
was widely known in the eighteenth century
through prints and copies by many who had
never been to Florence. Ingres first knew the
work through a copy in the studio of his
master in Toulouse, and the impact on his art,
before he had set foot in David's studio, was
decisive. Typically, Ingres saw beyond the
surface of the copy to the essential image,
and he constantly re-used elements of
the *Madonna della Sedia* in many of his works,
sometimes inserting the whole composition in
miniature like a signature.

soon to become portrait painter to the courts of Europe, but still, at the time of Ingres's arrival at David's studio in 1797, a history painter of outstanding promise whose poetic style seemed to mark a break with his master's classic prose. Ingres particularly admired this period of Gérard's work, the pale, sharp-edged *Psyche*, his favourite painting by Gérard, the Romantic *Ossian* of 1801, the source of his own *Ossian* (Plate III) of 1811, and the early portraits whose attenuated elegance and facial mannerisms recall the sinuous ideal imposed by Ingres on *Madame Rivière* (Plate I), *Mademoiselle Rivière* (Plate 9) and *Madame de Senonnes* (Plate 26). It is not essential to place Ingres in the fringe lunacy of the Primitifs, a group of mystics in the following of David who affected archaic manners in their life and work, to explain the pre-Raphaelite elegance of these works by Ingres and his contemporaries. Gérard and Girodet were associated by critics with Perugino and Leonardo and, although critics are not always a sure guide to the intentions of the artist, the evidence of French Neo-Classic painting suggests a quattrocentist influence extending well beyond the confines of the esoteric Primitifs. Perugino and Leonardo, represented in the Louvre, were then the most accessible of the many artists in the late quattrocento who had been influenced by the linear mannerism of Tuscan art between Filippo Lippi and Raphael. Botticelli, who exemplifies the style to twentieth-century eyes, was deemed too obscure to count in the early nineteenth century. The facial types and linear emphasis in the art of Ingres and his contemporaries, and the quattrocentist use of gold in *Venus Wounded* (Plate 4) relate to these painters' known interest in the art of the early Renaissance in Italy. Neither Perugino nor Leonardo, however, could have competed with Raphael as the main source of Ingres's ideal, but critics rarely mentioned Perugino without Raphael in mind. They were disturbed by the interest of French artists in the Peruginesque aspect of Raphael, which was less admired in 1800 than it was to be in 1850. Academic orthodoxy in the eighteenth century had linked Raphael with his Roman and Bolognese successors, encouraging students to look at him with eyes accustomed to the Grand Manner and to dismiss his easel paintings in which, as Reynolds said, 'he never was able to conquer perfectly that dryness, or even littleness of manner which he inherited from his master.' But in the nineteenth century, as the Bolognese fell from critical grace, Raphael changed company to become the last and greatest of the primitives. Ingres valued the naivety of the primitives, contrasting them with the decadence of artists after Raphael. Believing, however, that the genius of Raphael lay in his discovery of a prelapsarian ideal, as absolute as a law of nature, he always imposed a Raphaelesque grace on the naivety he admired in the earlier artists. Ingres's *Romulus* (Plate 30) of 1812, derived in part from Mantegna's *Triumphs of Julius Caesar*, transformed the solemn manner of the original with a rhythm and sweetness which corresponded to an idea of the early Raphael at a time when his style blended elements of Leonardo and Perugino, and if *Roger Freeing Angelica* has a source in Italian art it is not to be found in Cimabue, as was suggested at the time, but in such works by Raphael as the *St. George* in Washington.

David idealized the heroism of life, Ingres idealized its grace. David's art was by no means exempt from grace, but his grace was fresh and natural at the point where Ingres was mannered. At its best, David's art was public and heroic, rooted in the seicento with side glances at the Antique and the High Renaissance, while Ingres was *intimiste* and showed his loathing for the conventions of seventeenth-century Italian painting, on which the Classicism of the eighteenth century was based. Like many radicals Ingres thought he was reverting to a classic norm. He never wholly realized the uniqueness of his achievement. Only in the post classical world of the mid-nineteenth century did Ingres's attempt to reassert the authority of Antique myth and history attain classic status and then at the expense of David, who was demoted from the ranks of true classics.

Between his brilliant début in 1801 and his appearance at the Salon of 1806, Ingres changed course to become the first of the great radicals of nineteenth-century French art. The exhibition of his portraits of the Rivière family (Plates I, 8, 9), his *Self-portrait* (Plate 11) and *Napoleon on the Imperial Throne* (Plate 6) opens the series of famous occasions in the history of modern art—the appearance of Delacroix's *Death of Sardanapalus*, Courbet's *Burial at Ornans*, Manet's *Olympia* and the first Impressionist exhibition—when the new and unexpected raised a public outcry. Ingres, after fifteen years of praise and encouragement, was upset but unrepentant. 'Art could well do with reforming', he wrote from Italy, 'and I would like to be the revolutionary who does it.' He recognized the gulf between his pictures and those of his contemporaries: 'and the more I press forward, the less my pictures will resemble theirs.' In a mood of humiliated fury, Ingres turned his thoughts to the course work for the Ecole de Rome, tormented by ambition yet uncompromising in his determination to be *avant garde*.

The paintings dating from Ingres's association with the Ecole de Rome form a distinct group in his work. The regulations of the course required the student to paint studies of the nude figure and a historic composition, invariably taken at this period from ancient myth and history. Ingres thought of a number of motifs giving scope to the depiction of female grace and male beauty which would impose themselves upon the Paris judges and revenge the débâcle of his reception at the Salon. He considered a figure of Venus and a *Hercules among the Pygmies*, a projection of his desire to crush his enemies in Paris, but eventually submitted the so-called *Valpinçon Bather* (Plate 18) and *Oedipus and the Sphinx* (Plate 16), a more fitting image of intellectual conquest than the brute force of Hercules. He began work on a first version of *Stratonice*, but chose instead, for his historic set piece, an episode from the *Iliad* in which Thetis begs Zeus to intervene in the Trojan wars on behalf of her son, Achilles (Plate 29). This subject allowed the artist to contrast the masculine strength of Zeus with the limp charms of Thetis, thus combining the idealized types of beauty associated with Venus and Hercules while exaggerating and intensifying their characters in the same composition. This period in which Ingres's thoughts were concentrated on subjects which allowed him to paint single nude figures culminated in *The Grande Odalisque* (Plate 34), completed in 1814 as a pendant to *The Sleeping Woman*, a reclining nude bought by Joachim Murat, then King of Naples, in 1809 and subsequently lost. Despite the eccentricity which critics at the Académie and the Salon found detestable, this group of works could not have been conceived without the conditions imposed on students at the Ecole de Rome. *The Valpinçon Bather*, *Oedipus*, *The Birth of Venus* (Plate 63) and *The Grande Odalisque* are all essentially academic studies of single nude figures, transformed by Ingres's intuitive exaggeration of the character and by his refusal to employ conventional technique. Despising the majority of contemporary artists, Ingres readily sacrificed the lessons of David and the Ecole to the magic of Raphael; the light which breaks on the angles of the Valpinçon bather's back is no longer the dramatic academic light which moulds the body of his prize-winning *Male Torso* (Plate 2) of 1800 but a new, subtle poetry of tones which he had discovered in Italian art.

When his scholarship ended Ingres decided to remain in Rome where conditions of patronage under the French government of occupation were favourable to a resident French artist. He took part in the redecoration of the Quirinal Palace for the Emperor Napoleon in 1811–12 and was in demand among the colony of French officials and administrators and their families as a portrait painter. Murat and his wife Caroline, sister of the emperor, became his chief patrons after their purchase of *The Sleeping Woman*, and Ingres went to their court at Naples c. 1813 to prepare a portrait of the queen and another of her family. The Murats acquired *The Betrothal of Raphael*, the first of his historic genre pictures, and commissioned a pendant to *The Sleeping Woman*, *The Grande Odalisque*, which Ingres completed but did not deliver owing to the collapse of the Napoleonic empire in 1814. The withdrawal of the French from Italy was a severe blow to Ingres, who lost his clientèle and was left with projects unpaid for and unfinished on his hands. He was now obliged to make a living for himself and his wife, whom he had married in 1813 as his circumstances were improving, by drawing portraits of the hordes of

fig. 2 François-Pascal-Simon GRANGER
Scipio Receives his Son from the Envoys of Antiochus
Paris, Musée du Louvre

Granger won the Grand Prix de Rome in 1800 with this picture in competition with Ingres, who shared second place. The indefinite setting, lost in the gloom of theatrical light and shade, represents an aspect of academic art against which Ingres was later to react strongly. Some artists felt that Ingres's sharply detailed and more gracious version, destroyed in 1871 during the Commune, should have won the prize, but the award by an academic jury to Granger was unanimous.

English tourists who crowded back to liberated Rome.

Trained to cherish the status of High Art, Ingres, like many of his fellow history painters, associated the portrait painter's career with failure and the second rate. Of a total of over 450 known portrait drawings, the large majority dates from the years 1806 to 1824, when Ingres was obliged to exploit this talent to supplement his income. Commissioned portraits are more finished than those done for friends, and the portraits dating from before 1834 are more sparing in technique than the later series when Ingres often used an added white. From the neatly hatched and outlined drawings of before 1806 such as the profile portrait in the Fogg Art Museum (Plate 1), Ingres evolved the classic type of his first Italian period in which the outlines became light and free and costumes were suggested with a minimum of racing lines and pale hatching. Heads are more carefully observed than costume, with subtle indications of tonality, strongest in the salient features of the eyes, nostrils, lips and hair, delicate in the bone structure where the fine grain of the paper gives texture to the shading. Ingres's portrait drawings recall a type more typically English than French, associated with Henry

fig. 3 Jean-Louis LANEUVILLE
Portrait of the Conventionnel Louis Legendre
formerly Paris, Cailleux Collection

This portrait, exhibited at the Salon of 1795,
typifies the liveliness and spontaneity which
were the hallmark of intimate portraiture in the
late eighteenth century in France. Ingres was
lastingly influenced by the genre.

Edridge or Richard Cosway, whose wife made a
small stir in the Paris art world of Ingres's youth. Ingres
was free and lively, however, where the English artists
were punctilious. The style recalls outline engraving.
Ingres etched a few of his own portraits, and he might
have known Cosway's and Edridge's originals through
imported prints which, before 1814, would have been
a French artist's only access to recent developments in
English portraiture.

By the time Ingres settled in Florence in 1820,
tempted by the promises of clients, he had mastered the
conventions which separated his private from his public
portrait style. The intimate portraits, intended for the
sitter's family and friends, derived from David's conceit
of showing his subjects turning with a smile as if interrupted by the spectator in a characteristic occupation.
The variations on this bond of intimacy not only tell us
about the status of the sitter, but also about the character and sometimes the identity of the individuals for
whom the portrait was intended. Sitters do not smile at
the world at large. Public portraits rarely smile, and
Monsieur Rivière and Monsieur Leblanc, now smiling
at millions annually in Paris and New York, intended

to confine their affability to the family circle. Just as
the only possible viewers of Velásquez's *Las Meninas*
could have been Philip IV of Spain and his consort,
Queen Mariana, Ingres's early *Self-portrait* (Plate 11),
was clearly intended originally for his friend Gilibert,
whose portrait was on the easel. When Ingres transformed the *Self-portrait* in later life, erasing the picture
on the easel and giving himself a bland, Raphaelesque
manner, he altered this private relationship into a
portrait of the artist as a public figure. Laneuville's
Portrait of Legendre (fig. 3) of the 1790s, showing the
sitter engaged in conversation with the spectator, invites
comparison with Ingres's *Monsieur Bertin* (Plate 51) of
forty years later. Although the pose which Ingres adopted
was inspired by the sight of Bertin listening to the conversation of a friend and although the artist probably
never saw the earlier portrait, this treatment is linked
to Laneuville and the late eighteenth century by the
idea of the portrait as an image of a person caught in a
moment of intimacy by his friends or family.

By 1830, however, Ingres had evolved a more original, less intimate style of portraiture, influenced, perhaps, by his admiration for the work of Titian, in which
he depicted the public image of his subject, using conventions of space, pose, looks and gestures to define the
moral and physical distance between the model and
the viewer. Some of these pictures, exhibited in public
or distributed in prints and copies, were intended for
the public eye, but Ingres increasingly used these conventions to portray anyone in official positions, even
when the portraits were not intended for public exhibition. Amédée-David de Pastoret (Plate 45), formerly a
diplomat of the Empire from a recently ennobled
family, was doubtless flattered to see himself portrayed
as an official of the Bourbon Restoration, scowling at
his public. The distinction between the private and the
public genre is, therefore, blurred by self-esteem. Ingres
first thought of painting Bertin as a public figure, but,
finding the imagery inappropriate, he reserved the pose
for his *Portrait of the Comte Molé* (Plate 54), and chose a
more intimate solution, to the disappointment of Bertin's
daughter, who would have preferred to see her father
as a *grand seigneur*. Confronted by the duc d'Orléans,
however, Ingres did not hesitate in the choice of his
convention (Plate 55). His experience of public portraits immediately suggested the simple military pose
rising into a dramatic emptiness which introduced a
new effect of spare elegance into nineteenth-century
official portraits.

As Ingres turned to portrait drawing in the Restoration for a source of income, he also found a profitable
career in painting pictures of historic genre. In his
days at the Capuchins he had been in contact with the
pupils of David, provincials, like himself, from the
south of France, who pioneered post classical history
as a genre in art. Ingres and his colleagues did not
take the heroic classicism of David for a model, but

instead looked to the detailed realism and precious finish of seventeenth-century Dutch art, influenced, as were those artists who sent landscapes, genre pictures and interiors to the Salons in increasing numbers during the First Empire, by the fashionable tendency to collect the *petits maîtres* of the United Provinces. Ingres's commissions and his course work for the Ecole de Rome postponed his first attempt at historic genre until 1814 when he composed *The Betrothal of Raphael* for Queen Caroline Murat. The genre was popular among members of the Imperial family who followed the *rentiers* and aristocrats of the *ancien régime* in their passion for Dutch art, but even after the Bonapartes had gone the politics of the Restoration enormously increased the demand for episodes of French history which might tie present loyalties to tradition. The royalist comte de Blacas bought Ingres's pleasant tributes to Henri IV and François I and the duque de Alba and the marquis de Pastoret commissioned Ingres to illustrate the efforts of their ancestors in suppressing revolt and restoring monarchy. Apart from the duque de Alba's commission to commemorate the brutality of his ancestor in the service of Philip II of Spain, these subjects were congenial to Ingres who, after twenty years of academic work, was anxious to extend his range. 'Reading Montfaucon,' he noted, 'I am convinced that the history of ancient France from the time of St. Louis and others would be a new vein to exploit; that costumes were then very attractive and some of them resemble the fashions of the Greeks; that even those which appear bizarre only do so on account of the weak art by which they have come down to us; that beautiful heads, beautiful bodies, beautiful attitudes, beautiful gestures are timeless. A history painter who makes a speciality of this period would command resources of great beauty as far as art is concerned and of great interest to our contemporaries whose hearts are not moved by Achilles and Agamemnon, handsome as they are, as they are moved by St. Louis, Philippe de Valois, Louis le Jeune and so many others. One must admit that love of religion, which animated these old warriors, gives their pictures a mystic atmosphere which is simple and imposing particularly in the women and even in the men. The conclusion to be drawn from this is that I must follow this path as the right one and content myself with exploiting the Greeks, without whom there can be no safety, and amalgamating them, so to speak, with this new genre. This is how I can become an innovator and give my works a character of beauty hitherto unknown outside the works of Raphael. I am certain that if Raphael had been required to paint pictures of Greek subjects, he would interest us far less.'

The passage confirms the evidence of Ingres's work in the period of the Restoration. Between 1812 and 1826, Ingres painted no significant work inspired by the Antique. On the other hand, this was the period of

The Betrothal of Raphael, Don Pedro de Toledo, Roger Freeing Angelica, Philip V and the duke of Berwick, Henri IV Receiving the Spanish Ambassador, The Death of Leonardo, The Interior of the Sistine Chapel, The Entry of the Dauphin, Aretino in the Studio of Tintoretto and *Aretino and the Envoy of Charles V.* Apart from *The Entry of the Dauphin* (Plate 36) and *Philip V and the duke of Berwick* these subjects were evidently of Ingres's choosing, inspired sometimes by the Salon pictures of his friends in Paris but also illustrating his own personal ambition, affections and desires. Like Delacroix discovering elements of Homeric Greece among the Arabs of Morocco, Ingres found the beauties of Antiquity in Medieval and Renaissance history. Sully and Henri IV reminded him of Pylades and Orestes, and his early drawing on the theme of Alexander, Campaspe and Apelles, now in Montauban, foreshadowed the later theme of Cardinal Bibiena, his niece and Raphael.

Apart from an echo of the Neo-Classical in the geometry of *The Death of Leonardo* (Plate 31) and the first version of *Don Pedro de Toledo*, the eclecticism of Ingres's sources and his painstaking but spirited touch imitated from van Mieris and Teniers make it difficult at first to reconcile these polished miniatures with prevailing attitudes to the Antique. Ingres, however, attributed the perfection of Greek art not to formal values but to the naive realism of the artist. In his eyes, Giotto was more true to the Antique than Rubens. Ingres himself, however, was not a naive realist; for him the superiority of Raphael and the Greeks lay in the exercise of discretion and selection before the crudity of nature, like Zeuxis, composing his famous Venus from the amalgamated beauties of Crotona. The act of tidying up the appearance of reality allowed Ingres to idealize the human form more than he was prepared to admit. Like David, Vien, Vincent and most of the critics and artists of the period, Ingres did not accept that art should represent what did not or could not exist in nature. Beauty, style and the works of Raphael could all be found in nature by the discriminating eye, and no theory of beauty was so contested by the theorists of French Neo-Classicism as the abstract *beau idéal* proposed by Winckelmann. Quatremère de Quincy, who was almost alone in France in following the German into the realms of his ideal, was angrily interrupted by Ingres when he tried to explain his theory to the Académie in 1827. 'Do you think I send you to the Louvre to find something commonly called the *beau idéal*, something not in nature?' Ingres asked his pupils. 'That is the sort of rubbish which, when times are bad, contributes to the decadence of art. I send you to the Louvre to learn from the antiquities how to see nature, because they are themselves nature. You must live with them, absorb them. Do the same with the art of all great centuries.'

The diffusion of the search for strong sensation from the study of the Antique into other genres was charac-

fig. 4 Eugène DELACROIX
Study of Paganini
Washington, Phillips Collection

Delacroix's study of Paganini uses the
qualities of the sketch to express the passionate
virtuosity of the violinist. Ingres detested the
violence of brushwork and subject matter
adopted by young artists during the
Restoration, and comparison with his own
earlier portrait of Paganini (Plate 41) shows
his less frenzied and more sensitive approach
to the expressive qualities of art.

teristic of European Neo-Classicism. The history of the
Middle Ages, descriptions of the orient and the poetry of
Ossian gave new vitality to the romance associated
with ancient Greece. Ingres's languid *Odalisque with
the Slave* (Plate 52) throws her arm backwards like the
statue of Ariadne in the Louvre, transformed into the
type of Ingres's limp, sensuous ideal and transported
into the imagined world of Hugo's *Orientales* or Tom
Moore's *Lalla Rookh*. The orient remained the living
image of ancient Greece throughout the nineteenth
century, inspiring some of Ingres's best work after his
return from Italy in 1824. In other respects, however,
Ingres, like a number of David's pupils in the 1820s, took
fright at the collapse of the master's system, restricted
his inspiration to more conventional limits, and

opposed further innovation in art. As middle age
approached during the early years of the Restoration,
he was increasingly troubled by the spectre of High
Art, reminding him of the unkept promise of his youth,
and while Géricault, in Paris, was planning to establish
his reputation with a spectacular Salon picture, Ingres,
still in Italy, let the authorities know that he was also
anxious to paint something on a grander scale than
portraits and cabinet pictures. The French ambassador
in Rome, the comte de Blacas, replied to his request in
1817 with a commission for *Christ Giving the Keys of
Heaven to St. Peter* (Plate 46). Ingres's thoughts now
turned more directly to Raphael than before. The
composition which he completed for the ambassador in
1820 was taken from Raphael's cartoon for *Feed My Sheep*,
but the delicate relation between the drapery of St.
Peter and the robe of Christ in Raphael's work was
turned by Ingres into a startling fusion at the centre of
the picture, giving soaring emphasis to Christ's gesture
and strengthening the bond between Christ and the
first vicar of the Christian church. The lapidary sym-
bolism of the motif, the highly sculpted, stone-like
moulding of the central group, placed on a rock, gives
a remote, mystic tone to the solemn episode without
offending academic standards of naturalism and propriety, and the work seems to have pleased everyone
who saw it. Ingres could not send it to the Paris Salon
as he hoped, but as the news of its success reached
France, he received a commission from the authorities
at Montauban to paint an altarpiece on the theme of
Louis XIII dedicating his kingdom to the Virgin
(Plate 47). After eighteen years of exile in Italy, Ingres
accompanied this finished work to Paris, where it was
the outstanding success of the 1824 Salon. *The Vow of
Louis XIII* pleased the supporters of Classicism and
Romanticism without appearing to belong to either
school and confirmed Ingres as the foremost religious
painter of the day. Despite his refusal to take part in
decorating the newly built or newly restored churches
of Paris during the July Monarchy of the Orléans king,
Louis Philippe, he was well placed with architects and
government officials to recommend pupils in his place
so that by a mixture of accident and shrewd calculation
on the part of pupils with an eye on the main chance,
his studio became associated with the revival of religious painting in the first half of the century. Ingres's
own mind, however, did not distinguish sharply between the religious and the secular. His interest in
religious subjects was caused by the demands of
Restoration patronage. When the moral climate had
changed with the fall of Murat in Naples, he had tried
to recover his erotic *Sleeping Woman* by offering an
austere religious work of the same dimension in ex-
change. Angels and cupids, Madonnas and odalisques
fused together in his thoughts. Raphael's *Madonna della
Sedia* and Raphael's mistress, seen together in *Raphael
and the Fornarina* (Plate 33), are the same person. His

celebrity, as he once remarked, dated from the exhibition of an ex-voto, *The Vow of Louis XIII*, which proved to him that what mattered was not what you did but how you did it.

In his student days, Ingres had identified with Raphael against the orthodoxy of the Académie, but, in middle age, as his anger turned on the radicalism and Romanticism of Delacroix, he adhered more closely to academic tradition. His *Apotheosis of Homer* (Plate 48) of 1827 takes its place with Stendhal's *Salon de 1824* and Hugo's preface to *Cromwell* as one of the great manifestoes in the debate between the ancients and the moderns, the Classicists and the Romantics, of the 1820s: yet Ingres did not sustain the polemic with the conviction of a true classic. In his choice of forty-two *immortels* acknowledging their debt to Homer, Ingres mixed a host of conventional classics like Racine, whom he detested, with some Romantic favourites like Dante, Tasso, Shakespeare and Camoëns. The calm symmetry owes nothing to contemporary Classicism but was derived from the *stanze* of Raphael, who was included among the privileged company of the ancients, led by Apelles towards the throne of Homer. By the time he had completed the second version of *The Apotheosis of Homer* (Plate 49) in 1865, Ingres's commitment to convention had become more resolute. Shakespeare, Tasso and Camoëns were omitted as too Romantic, but there were no second thoughts about the admission of Racine and, forgetting that he had once accused David of deceiving him and leading him astray, he included his master holding the young Ingres by the hand like Apelles leading Raphael.

As Ingres realigned his taste in the 1820s in favour of the classics, the number of historical genre pictures fell sharply. The enthusiasm with which Delacroix and his friends followed Bonington's spirited adaptation of the genre (fig. 5) encouraged the growing conviction that the Middle Ages were Romantic property. Yet the experience of historic genre had a lasting influence on Ingres's interest in local colour, which is a striking feature in all his history paintings after 1820, and he retained a fondness for Medieval and Renaissance history which did not altogether fit his public image. 'To tell the truth', he confessed to Gilibert, after seeing a performance of Dumas's ultra-Romantic *Henri III et sa cour*, '—but not a word of this to anyone since, as leader of the classics, I can't afford to let it get around—I admit that I was pleased. For me, it is a great deal to see men painted as they are. Besides, the production as far as costumes and customs were concerned, was terrifyingly accurate.'

Ingres reacted to the decline of Classicism in art by returning to his work associated with the Ecole de Rome. *Stratonice* and the *Venus* were taken up again in the early 1820s; *Oedipus* reworked was sent to the Salon of 1827; *The Valpinçon Bather* became the centre of an earlier version of *The Turkish Bath* (Plate 70); and *The Sleeping*

fig. 5 Richard BONINGTON
Henri IV and the Spanish Ambassador
London, Wallace Collection

Exhibited at the Salon of 1827 and clearly inspired by Ingres's composition (Plate 37) on the same theme, which had been inspired, in turn, by Revoil and which had been exhibited at the previous Salon and which, this lively picture demonstrates the leading rôle of Ingres and the 'troubadours' in the development of historic genre.

Woman reappeared as *The Odalisque with the Slave* (Plate 52). This was the pattern of Ingres's Classicist reaction to the Romanticism of Paris for the last forty years of his life. Conscious that academic studies of the nude would not be acceptable as complete works of art, he added to the originals, giving extra prominence to the *amorini* at the feet of Venus, adding figures to the new versions of *The Sleeping Woman* and *The Valpinçon Bather* and putting a terrified observer into the picture of *Oedipus* to give drama to the elegantly posed Roman model.

As the supposed heir to the classical tradition, Ingres's place in the squabbles of the 1820s was anomalous. Delacroix and the Romantics admired his work at this period, while the critics of the old guard never came to terms with his Italianate alternative to the Classicism of David and criticized the forced mannerisms of *St. Symphorien* (Plate 53), exhibited in 1834, with severity. Ingres, unfairly blaming the Romantic press for his humiliation at the Salon, applied successfully for the directorship of the Ecole de Rome and returned to voluntary exile in Italy, determined more than ever to assert the prestige of Greece in opposition to the barbarism of modern art. 'I hope to be able to work seriously at Rome,' he wrote, 'and to treat subjects after my own heart, that is to say, inspired by the heroic annals of those astonishing, god-like peoples of antiquity.'

When in 1834 the duc d'Orléans commissioned Ingres to paint a pendant to Delaroche's *Assassination of the duc de Guise* he might reasonably have expected an

fig. 6 Anne-Louis GIRODET
Bacchante
Paris, Musée du Louvre, Cabinet des Dessins

This drawing, signed and dated 1812, derives ultimately from the Antique *Ariadne* in the Louvre, but the general similarity with Ingres's lost *Sleeping Woman*, which it postdates by four years, is evident and perhaps there was a common prototype. The drawing, a sort of female Endymion, is typical of Girodet, and the elegant, sinuous mannerism of the type profoundly affected Ingres's style in, for instance, *The Odalisque with the Slave* (Plates V and 52).

episode from the history of the Orléans family, but in view of Ingres's reactionary humour after the failure of *St. Symphorien*, the duc had to content himself with *Antiochus and Stratonice* (Plate 61), not the discarded original of 1808, which was half-size, but a smaller version scaled down to match the format of the Delaroche. The composition of the first version, derived from Girodet, was basically retained in the later painting, but comparison between the drawing (Plate 10) and the Orléans picture (Plate 61) shows how Ingres's experience of historic genre had toned down the mannerism of his early work. The bare interior in the drawing, dominated by its arabesque of foreground figures, was transformed in the later version into a plausibly Pompeian atrium. The remnant of the debt to Girodet, the sweet, affected mannerism of his style, seems almost intrusive in this peepshow realism and was not retained when Delaroche's pupils turned to *Stratonice* in the late 1840s for an anecdotal, anti-heroic, anti-Davidian model for the treatment of Antique themes. Despite the formal geometry of furniture and columns, borrowed from *Stratonice*, works like Gérôme's *King Candaulus* have more in common with the photographic intimacy of Alma-Tadema than with the Neo-Classical dream-world of Girodet.

The appearance of *Stratonice* in Paris in 1840 repeated the sensation of *The Vow of Louis XIII*. The painting was privately exhibited in the Palais Royal as Ingres refused to exhibit at the Salon after the reception of *St. Symphorien*, but everyone who counted saw the picture, and the press reviews were filled with rapture.

On his triumphal return from Rome in 1841 he began the portrait of the duc d'Orléans, finishing it by May of the following year when he put it on exhibition in his studio. The death of the duc two months later when his horses bolted drew Ingres closer to the Orléans family, and he was chosen by Louis Philippe to design the stained glass for the commemorative chapel built on the spot where the king's eldest son had died. This was followed by a commission to design the windows for the royal chapel at Dreux in 1844.

Although the portrait of the duc d'Orléans was his last important male portrait, Ingres was persuaded, in the decade after his return to Paris in 1841, to undertake a number of portraits of society hostesses, beginning with that of the vicomtesse d'Haussonville (Plate VI) in 1845 and ending with the *Portrait of Madame Moitessier* (Plate VIII), finished in 1856. The artifice of drapery and the elegance of pose of the early portraits were succeeded in the later commissions by a greater realism in the accessories and a casual snapshot quality combined with a new statuesque grandeur derived partly from Antique art and partly from Ingres's experience of public portraiture as he attempted to raise the simple portrait to the status of history painting.

Portraits and stained glass, however, kept Ingres from the great business of the moment, for in 1839 he had entered an agreement with the duc de Luynes to provide a pair of murals for his château at Dampierre, but, owing to Paris commitments, work could not begin until 1843. Ingres, who shared his generation's nostalgia for a lost Utopia, probably chose himself the contrast of *The Age of Gold* (Plate 62) and *The Age of Iron*. Nineteenth-century Paris, disrupted by a century of intermittent violence after 1789, found the contrast between war and peace particularly affecting. Ingres's ideal of primeval harmony finds an echo in the novels of George Sand, in Michelet's writings and in the idealism of the Fourierists, who supported Jean-Jacques Rousseau's noble savage in opposition to the pessimism of Hobbes and Baudelaire, which seemed confirmed by developments in evolutionary theory. Ingres's scheme was not an academic illustration of a text, as the idea of the Golden Age as a time of family bliss is not found in Hesiod, Ingres's ostensible source, but, rather, it was an emotional and personal response to the Iron Age of contemporary Paris.

After a brilliant start, the 1840s ended disastrously for Ingres. His official work was checked by the Revolution of 1848 when, for the second time in his career, his commissions were interrupted in mid-stream by the fall of the régime. *The Birth of Venus* (Plate 63), finished on commission after forty years, was left in Ingres's possession by its new owner, and the work at Dampierre, suspended during the Revolution, was abandoned in a half finished state following the shock of his wife's death in 1849. In a century of *fa presto* Ingres's facility to paint and draw astonished his contemporaries, but his chronic hesitations in composition and moods of nervous inactivity, which grew worse with age, made it increasingly difficult for him to finish his commissions. In his seventieth year, unsure either of himself or of his patrons, Ingres reconsidered his attitude to the sale and exhibition of his work.

The Paris Salon was the best outlet available to Ingres for the sale of pictures. With a number of less important exhibitions, the Salon allowed artists to dispense with patronage by offering their work on the open market. Although the general character of the exhibitions was ultimately decided by the buyers, the system encouraged innovation and a number of new movements, the fashion for historic genre, for instance, began in the Salon with artists searching for a speciality. Ingres recognized the commercial value of the Salon. He detested the institution of the jury, which prevented artists who had been refused a place from putting up their work for sale in the major art market and, thus, was one of the most forthright advocates of the free Salon in 1848. Ingres himself, however, hardly ever picked up a brush without a previous commission. He occasionally used the Salon as an outlet for a commission which went wrong, like *The Grande Odalisque*, or for a school piece, such as *Oedipus*, but, in general, his exhibitions at the Salon were meant to advertise his talent, not to sell his art. When the press was hostile the Salon lost its *raison d'être* for him, and he finally withdrew altogether. Instead of offering his work through dealers or at the Salon, Ingres worked in a close relationship with his patrons which allowed him influence in the choice of subject and which was instrumental, through the friendship of influential protectors like Marcotte and the Prince Napoleon-Joseph, in bringing him public honours without parallel in the history of French art. Yet Ingres came out of the crisis of 1848–49 determined to accept no more commissions but to work on his own initiative and offer finished pictures for sale to patrons at exhibitions in his studio. In 1851 he turned to his stock of tried ideas and unfinished canvases and set to work with new energy, helped by pupils, on his independent course. In the following year, on the advice of friends, Ingres remarried. He accepted one last public commission, in 1853, for a ceiling in the Hôtel de Ville, Paris, finishing it within the year, and on the occasion of the Paris World Fair of 1855 he relaxed his refusal to appear in state exhibitions, sending forty-three of his paintings and twenty-five of his designs for stained glass to the section of international art. As in 1824 and 1840, influential patrons seized the chance to honour their friend and protégé and, despite a few inevitable squibs of resentment provoked by his colossal reputation, the episode marked Ingres's public apotheosis.

After spending half of his life opposing the Académie Ingres changed in mid-career and, until his death in 1867, championed his official colleagues against the

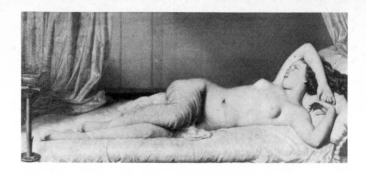

fig. 7 Eugène-Emmanuel AMAURY-DUVAL
Psyche
Riom, Musée Mandet

Amaury-Duval produced a number of nudes in the 1860s (see fig. 8) derived ostensibly from Ingres. This picture combines borrowings from *The Grande Odalisque* (Plate 34) and *The Odalisque with the Slave* (Plates V and 52), with a naivety and tempered naturalism characteristic of Amaury-Duval.

state. He offered to give evidence in court in support of Henri Rochefort's claim that the Louvre pictures had been overcleaned, he criticized the decision to disperse the items from the Campana collection which had been bought for France, and he published a denunciation of the government decree of 1863 ending the responsibility of the Académie in state education and diminishing its rôle in running the annual Salons. The aplomb with which he became the champion of orthodoxy, as uncompromising in his new rôle as Thomas à Becket at the archbishopric, alienated the sympathy of the radical opposition, and Realist and Romantic critics, wearied by the great Panjandrum of the Institut, caricatured his art unsparingly, as flat, Chinese and unimaginative. None of Ingres's early critics ever approached the desperate silliness of Théophile Silvestre or the blank response of Thoré and the Goncourts.

The nude studies of his Roman youth, however, reworked during his later years into odalisques and goddesses, were idolatrously admired by the Parnassian poets, who followed Gautier back to an imagined Age of Gold in ancient Greece, and were copied by young artists searching for 'style' as the fashionable antidote to Realism in the 1850s. For these reasons, none of Ingres's work excited so much emotion in his lifetime as *The Source* (Plate 64), a reworking of an early study related to *The Birth of Venus*, which Ingres exhibited in his studio in 1856. While the pupils of Delaroche looked to Ingres for a model of historic realism, the pupils of François Picot, whose studio produced more Prix de Rome winners than any other, fifteen in forty years, looked to Ingres for a method of combining art and grace with academic standards in the modelling of single nude figures. The poses of the odalisques and *The Source*, passing into the international vocabulary of mild erotica, became a standard feature of every Salon

fig. 8 Eugène-Emmanuel AMAURY-DUVAL
The Birth of Venus
Lille, Musée des Beaux-Arts

Exhibited in 1863, this tall, angular, pale
Venus distinguishes itself precisely from the
plush charm of Ingres's prototype (Plate 63).
Amaury-Duval's *Venus* appeared in the
enthusiastic revival of erotic myth in French
art which began in the late 1850s largely
because of Ingres's example.

in the second half of the nineteenth century. Ingres's
pupil, Amaury-Duval, writing in the 1870s at the
height of the fashion for the graces of *The Source*,
claimed, with the superiority of the eye witness, that
Ingres had spoilt the naive charm of *The Birth of Venus*
and *The Source* by reworking them in old age. In 1863
Amaury-Duval exhibited his own pale, angular version
of Ingres's *Venus*, which seems to have been intended as
a comment on the loss. His wide-eyed *Psyche* (fig. 7) of
1867, derived from *The Odalisque with the Slave*, was per-

haps painted as a critique of Cabanel's immensely
successful *Birth of Venus* (Paris, Louvre) which sump-
tuously blends a formal debt to Ingres with the airs of
Clodion and Boucher and which stole the thunder from
Amaury-Duval's own *Venus* at the Salon of 1863. But
no one could mistake Amaury-Duval's pretty innocents
for Ingres's lush transformation of the real, and Cabanel
was rightly sensitive to a decorative element in Ingres's
treatment of the nude. Ingres was not, as Amaury-
Duval supposed, a naive realist who lost the freshness of
his vision in growing old. He moved habitually from
the realism of the first studies towards a personal ideal
in the finished work, but his early compositions, when
the influence of Girodet and Flaxman was strongest,
were more idealized than the later ones which increasingly responded to his preoccupation with nature. The
head of *The Source* is realistic by comparison with that of
Thetis or of Venus, while the stillness of the society
hostesses in the last portraits is, partly, the calm grandeur of a Greek ideal, partly, the stiff naturalism of a
daguerrotype. The charm of Ingres does not lie in the
naivety of the primitives whom he admired, but in the
juxtaposition of this naivety with an exaggerated
elegance of form which survived a century of naturalism
to become an influence in the *fin de siècle*. Proust's
duchesse de Guermantes, after imagining for years that
Ingres had been the worst of academics, discovered in
the 1890s that he had been a charming precursor of Art
Nouveau. This had already been implied by hostile
critics in the 1840s and 1850s, who described his art as
meaningless and abstract, but Ingres was never abstract
if that implies a conscious intention to separate the
subject from the form. Ingres's loathing of the *beau
idéal* of Winckelmann rose from a conviction that
line and colour should express the character of the
model and had no value of their own. Like the architects of the Baroque, Ingres went beyond his mastery of
classic art to invent an expressive language of broken
rules through which he gave external shape to the
tender, nostalgic, ambitious, sensuous and vengeful
desires possessing his imagination. The ideal which he
imposed upon his model, although it had its formal
origins in the art of Raphael and Girodet, was not a
cold perfection imported from elsewhere but a strongly
felt response to nature. He exaggerated the size and
lustre of women's eyes because he was giddily susceptible
to their charm. He recreated women in his art, dis-
tilling beauty from the reality which he saw, but not
intentionally departing from the realm of nature for, as
Baudelaire remarked in 1846, when he could still
distinguish the real Ingres from the legend, 'he loves
his women too much to wish to change them; he pays
attention to their slightest beauties with the severity of
a surgeon: he follows the slightest ripple of their outline
with the servility of a lover. *Angelica*, the two *Odalisques*
and the portrait of Mme. d'Haussonville are the pro-
duct of a deeply sensuous nature'.

Bibliography

Anyone studying Ingres is fortunate in the industry of Ingres studies, which makes him one of the most accessible artists in the history of art. In addition to the following list, the invaluable catalogue of the Petit Palais exhibition (Paris, 1967–68) and the volumes of the *Bulletin du Musée Ingres* should be consulted.

Amaury-Duval, E.-E., *L'atelier d'Ingres*. Paris, 1878.

Balze, R., *Ingres, son école, son enseignement*. Paris, 1880.

Blanc, C., *Ingres, sa vie, ses ouvrages*. Paris, 1870.

Boyer d'Agen, A.-J., *Ingres d'après une correspondance inédite*. Paris, 1909.

Courthion, P., *Ingres raconté par lui-même et par ses amis*. Geneva, 1947–48.

Debia, P., *Souvenirs intimes sur Ingres*. Montauban, 1868.

Delaborde, H., *Ingres, sa vie, ses travaux, sa doctrine*. Paris, 1870.

Lapauze, H., *Les dessins de J.-A.-D. Ingres*. Paris, 1901.

Lapauze, H., *Ingres, sa vie et son oeuvre*. Paris, 1911.

Lapauze, H., *Les portraits dessinés de J.-A.-D. Ingres*. Paris, 1903.

Lapauze, H., *Le roman d'amour de M. Ingres*. Paris, 1910.

Magimel, A., *Oeuvres de J. A. Ingres gravées au trait sur acier par A. Réveil, 1800–1850*. Paris, 1851.

Rosenblum, R., *Ingres*. New York, 1967.

Schlenoff, N., *Ingres, ses sources littéraires*. Paris, 1956.

Silvestre, T., *Histoire des artistes vivants*. Paris, 1855.

Ternois, D. and Camesasca, E., *Tout l'oeuvre peint d'Ingres*. Paris, 1971.

Wildenstein, G., *Ingres*. London, 1954.

(*opposite*)
I *Portrait of Madame Rivière*
PARIS, Musée du Louvre. 1805. Oil on canvas 116·5 × 81·7 cm. Unsigned.
The flood of pale drapery which conceals the semi-reclining pose, contrasting with the patches of bright colour in the shawl and the blue velvet of the cushions, seemed exaggerated and ill-conceived to the critics of the 1806 Salon. Chaussard felt that the artist had shown a lack of respect in painting a disordered portrait of Mme. Rivière, whom he knew and admired. But the disorder has its own *raison d'être* in the swirling eddies of the composition, picked up by the circular motif on the end of the couch and by the oval frame. Her pose was intended to complement the seated figure of her husband, but the intention has been obscured by the contrast between the discretion of his portrait and the luxury of hers.

1 *Profile Portrait of a Young Man*

CAMBRIDGE (MASSACHUSETTS), Fogg Art Museum (gift of John S. Newberry). c. 1797. Pencil on parchment with paper backing 6·8 cm. diameter. Signed: Ingres fils.

A number of charming profile heads dating from the 1790s survive. The genre, imitating the classical medallion, was common at the time; small portrait medallion profiles like this were engraved by a patent process as a cheap alternative to the miniature. The delicacy of touch and careful parallel shading with finely modelled passages from light to shade were characteristic of Ingres's drawing style while he was studying in Toulouse and help to date the portrait to c. 1797. After he arrived in Paris, Ingres seems to have abandoned the portrait profile in favour of the less formal three-quarter view and, as Dr. Naef has indicated, profile heads do not recur in his work apart from a short series dating from 1810–12.

(*opposite*)

II *Portrait of Charles-Joseph-Laurent Cordier*

PARIS, Musée du Louvre. Oil on canvas 90 × 69·5 cm. Signed: Ingres, Roma 1811.

Hans Naef identified the subject as a member of the French administration in Rome. Casually leaning against a ruined wall watching the storm clouds over Tivoli, like Granet at his parapet, Cordier turns to face the spectator. This portrait, commissioned by a government official, is understandably less informal than the portrait of Granet; Cordier's black, brass buttoned suit introduced a new note of sobriety and elegance into Ingres's male portraits.

2 *Male Torso*
PARIS, Ecole des Beaux-Arts. Oil on canvas 102 × 80 cm.
Unsigned.

This heroic study, painted in 1800, won first prize in the
competition for torso painting at the Ecole des Beaux-
Arts. Fourteen months after entering the Ecole, Ingres
demonstrated complete mastery in the academic science
of modelling the human figure in strong chiaroscuro.
The picture is built up from a warm, dark ground
which shows through the large areas of lightly painted
shadow, contrasting with the opaque highlights on the
model's right. Ingres abandoned this loose, thin, broken
brushwork and transparent shading after his arrival in
Italy in 1806, but the elegance of form, the Greek
profile and the expressive eye looking upwards to the
light are characteristic of the element of poetry which
tempered the realism of his mature style.

(*opposite top*)
3 *The Ambassadors of Agamemnon and the Chiefs of the Greek Army, Preceded by Heralds, Arrive at the Tent
of Achilles to Beg Him to Fight*
PARIS, Ecole des Beaux-Arts. Oil on canvas 110 × 155 cm. Signed: Ingres 1801.

The subject set for the Prix de Rome in 1801, *The Ambassadors of Agamemnon*, was taken from the
Iliad and offered excellent opportunity for figure drawing and strong contrast of facial expression.
Ingres made a subtle distinction between the muscular warriors on the right and the Praxitelean
grace of Patroclus and Achilles on the left. The poses of the figures recall several Antique statues
which could have been known to Ingres, either in the Louvre or else from casts and engravings.
Psychological expression was carefully observed without the exaggeration fashionable at the time.
In other respects also, Ingres departed from the academic tradition. He substituted a light,
mountainous view for the dark, indefinite backgrounds, favoured by competitors even though the
subject seems to indicate an interior scene, and the contrast between light and shadow is less
accentuated than was common at the time although this must be partly due to a repainting in the
1820s.

(*opposite bottom*)
4 *Venus Wounded by Diomedes*
BASEL, collection of Baron Robert von Hirsch. Oil on canvas 27 × 33 cm. c. 1805. Signed: Ingres.

This study, possibly related to a larger project which was never carried out, shows a debt to
Flaxman, whose line engravings attracted Gros, Girodet and the young Ingres among David's
pupils. The limp stylization of Venus and the sharply outlined profile of Iris are closer to the effect
of Flaxman than a finished composition, given body by close study from life, would have been.
Both the manes of the white horses and the chariot wheels are touched with gold and give the
composition a sense of archaic fantasy. Ingres modified his youthful excesses in later life: 'Péché de
jeunesse' he said apologetically when signing this work for its owner in the 1820s. His fondness for
the style of Flaxman, Girodet and Greek vase painting reasserted itself, however, on a number of
occasions as he turned again to his early works in later life.

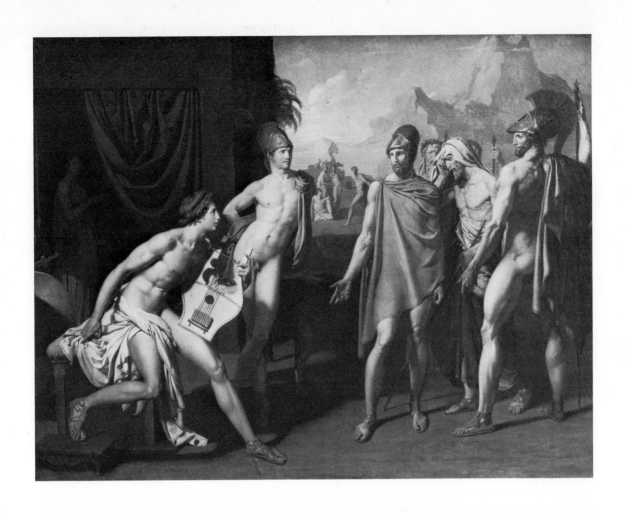

(*above left*)
5   *Bonaparte as First Consul*
LIÈGE, Musée des Beaux-Arts. Oil on canvas 227 × 147 cm. Signed: Ingres, an XII.

The traditional iconography of kingship associated with Rigaud and his state portraits of Louis XIV and Louis XV was abandoned by artists who portrayed Bonaparte with an imagery which justified authority by deeds. In August 1803 Bonaparte gave 300,000 francs to the municipality of Liège to rebuild the suburb of Amercoeur, bombarded by the Austrians in 1794. Ingres had received his commission for a portrait of the First Consul intended to remind the Liègeois of his projected generosity even before the grant had been made, and as Greuze had also been commissioned for a portrait of Bonaparte, both artists were granted a brief joint sitting with the First Consul by way of preparation. Ingres painted the costume and the body at his leisure, but the head, based on his usual rapid studies, was not painted from life and sits stiffly on the velvet costume, painted in fluent, blended strokes of gold and scarlet. The flat, unvarying surface of the wall and the flattened perspective of the floor disrupt the realism, but the eye wanders through the window to the view of the Cathedral of St. Lambert in Liège, destroyed in the bombardment, a vignette of Gothic spires and summer sky reminiscent of van Eyck.

(*above right*)
6   *Napoleon on the Imperial Throne*
PARIS, Musée de l'Armée. Oil on canvas 260 × 163 cm. Signed: Ingres, Pxit ANNO 1806.

Between the commission for the portrait of Bonaparte for Liège and this portrait for the Corps Législatif, the First Consul had been crowned emperor. Sensitive to the changed status of his model, Ingres created an image of imperial power which forms an extreme contrast with David's no less propagandist view of the legislating Bonaparte as a man who stayed up until the early hours of the morning drafting laws. The pose which Ingres used, originally associated with the Jupiter of Olympus by Phidias, was a stock image for gods and emperors well into the Middle Ages, making it difficult to be certain about Ingres's source. When it appeared at the Salon of 1806, the connections seen by artists and critics with Byzantine medals, religious statuary, Dürer, van Eyck and Charlemagne not only show the familiarity with the Middle Ages which Paris had acquired by 1806 but also suggest a situation in which Ingres might well have drawn upon a Medieval tradition. Charlemagne seems the best suggestion for a source, according to Francis Haskell, partly because

the comparison would have seemed so appropriate. Ingres shows the emperor holding the sceptre of King Charles V and the so-called Hand of Charlemagne in a pose which has been traced to portraits of Charlemagne in Montfaucon's published catalogue of antiquities. There is a connection, surely conscious, between the emperor's pose and the statuette on the head of the sceptre. Critics were probably right in attributing the conception of the portrait to a Gothic source, but it was not well received and Ingres's reputation took sixteen years to recover from the exhibition of this work.

(above)
7 *Portrait of Madame Aymon*
ROUEN, Musée des Beaux-Arts. Oil on canvas 59 × 49 cm. Signed: Ingres 1806.

The fame of this portrait dates from its entry into the art gallery at Rouen in 1870. Its history before that date and even the identity of the sitter are unknown. The title 'La Belle Zélie' was given to it at this time from that of a popular song. The open smile, which seems to belie the distance in her eyes, is not common in Ingres and shows the influence of David. The thin, free brushwork of the dress is characteristic of the early Ingres. The lines of the composition play effectively with the oval format, but the red of her shawl, the flat black of her hair and the blue of the sky give a strength of colour lacking in the more subtle harmonies of the almost contemporary portrait of Mlle. Rivière (Plate 9).

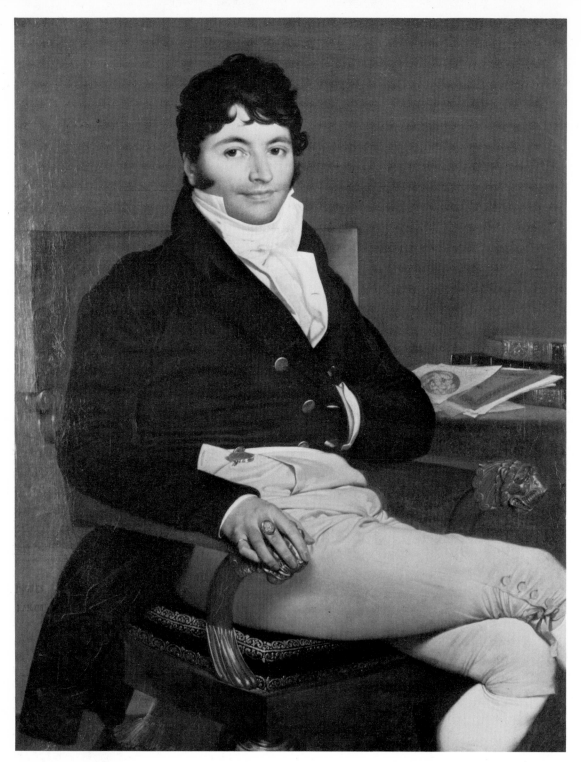

8 *Portrait of Philibert Rivière*
PARIS, Musée du Louvre. 1805. Oil on canvas 116 × 89 cm. Signed: Ingres l'an XIII.

Ingres exhibited three portraits (Plates I, 9) of the Rivière family with his self-portrait (Plate 11) in 1806. M. Rivière, sitting by his books and papers with an informality which recalls the portraits of David, smiles at the spectator. On the desk, Ingres placed a print after the *Madonna della Sedia* which reappears in his work like a signature, showing his characteristic devotion to Raphael well before his departure for Italy.

(*opposite*)
9 *Portrait of Mademoiselle Rivière*
PARIS, Musée du Louvre. 1805. Oil on canvas 100 × 70 cm. Signed: Ingres.

The oval fascination of the eyes and the gleaming scarlet of the lips against the pale face reveal the artist's response to this 'ravishing girl' of fifteen. Ingres resented the description of this work as 'Gothic'. The modifications of the features have no precise source apart from a general conception of beauty of varied origins and a desire on the part of the artist to draw attention to characteristic aspects of the beauty of his model by exaggerating them. The simple geometry of the pose, inter-

rupted by the arabesque of fur, the dark grass of the hillside giving contrast to the white dress and the salient of the distant landscape, isolating her head and shoulders and drawing attention to her face, are formally effective. The brushwork also has a life of its own, expressing light and texture with a thin liquid stroke, always stopping short of the over precious finish which can destroy the illusion it sets out to create.

10 *Antiochus and Stratonice*

PARIS, Musée du Louvre, Cabinet des Dessins. c. 1807. Pencil and brown wash on paper 29 × 40 cm. Unsigned.

Ingres turned to the popular theme of Antiochus's near-fatal passion for his step-mother in c. 1807 when he was considering various Antique themes for submission to his Paris judges. He began a painting half-life size but discontinued it, offering, in 1821, to complete it for a patron in Montauban. Ingres had hopes of sending it to the Salon of 1824, but the work was probably never completed and it is now known only from this study, dating from the project's inception c. 1807, which seems to have belonged to Ingres's friend Girodet. In the 1790s Girodet had composed a painting of the same subject, showing the doctor diagnosing the prince's illness which, on the evidence of a sketch now in Bayonne, was clearly the model for Ingres's version. The figure of Antiochus, in particular, recalls Girodet's limp ideal of beauty. Ingres retained the basic idea of this composition in the painting of the same subject (Plate 61) for the duc d'Orléans, which he completed in 1840.

(opposite)

11 *Self-portrait at the Age of Twenty-four*

CHANTILLY, Musée Condé. Oil on canvas 77 × 61 cm. Signed: Eff. J. A. Ingres Por Fit. Pa[r]is 1804.

Ingres exhibited this self-portrait at the Salon of 1806, where it was severely criticized. He repainted the canvas shortly before 1851, perhaps in preparation for the engraving by Reveil published in 1851, showing the portrait in its present state. Comparison between the early state, known from a photograph and a copy in Geneva, and its present appearance shows the change from the radicalism of youth in the first version to the conservatism of maturity. The first version was an introspective, intimate portrait of the artist, and, since it showed Ingres at work on a portrait of Gilibert, his childhood friend from Montauban, the picture was possibly painted for Gilibert or at least commemorates their friendship. The intensity of the artist's gaze in the first version is explained by the concentration of the artist on his model, the spectator, whom he is in the act of painting. The final picture is a portrait of the artist as a public figure; the canvas on his easel has been turned away from the spectator so the work in hand becomes indefinite and the artist's gaze modified to an amiable but somewhat blank expression. The hands are now posed with a Raphaelesque elegance, suggesting an element of self-identification, and the previous uncompromising juxtaposition of white coat and duster against a white canvas, which had shocked critics in 1806, was suitably modified. Between the first and last versions of this canvas the portrait changed to accord with Ingres's acquired status as a public eminence.

12 *Portrait of Madame Devauçay*

CHANTILLY, Musée Condé. Oil on canvas 76 × 59 cm. Signed: J. Ingres. Rom. 1807.

In Rome Ingres found patrons in the French colony of artists, diplomats and officials in the government of occupation. Shortly after his arrival in Rome, he received 500 francs for this portrait of the French ambassador's mistress. Again, Ingres made use of a strong rotary movement to hold the spectator's eye within the composition. The tonality is more restrained than in his previous female portraits. The dull yellow of her shawl over the dark velvet of her dress makes a subdued effect in keeping with her pallid features and demurely raised eyes, but the colour is saved from being dull by the splash of red and gold in the upholstery of the chair. Shortly before the Salon of 1833, Ingres recovered the portrait from Mme. Devauçay, then old and poor, and sold it for her to Frédéric Reiset.

13 *Portrait of François-Marius Granet*
AIX-EN-PROVENCE, Musée Granet. 1807. Oil on canvas 72 × 61 cm. Signed: J. A. Ingres.

Ingres and Granet both had studios in the Capuchin convent in Paris and later drew the Roman
landscape together. Ingres depicted Granet at a parapet, overlooking the Quirinal Palace, holding
a sketch book and turning round as if about to speak, with a gentle melancholy in his eyes. The
storm clouds giving contrast to the head add to the Romantic atmosphere of which Granet was
himself a master in his paintings of historic scenes set in dramatically lit interiors. It is ironic
that both Ingres and Granet became two of the warmest opponents of Romanticism in the 1830s.

(above left)
14 *Portrait of Lucien Bonaparte*
NEW YORK, collection of John Goelet. Pencil on paper 25 × 19 cm. Inscribed by another hand: Ingres.

Ingres probably met Lucien Bonaparte, Napoleon I's brother, through Guillon-Lethière, the director of the Ecole de Rome, who had been Lucien's artistic adviser during his embassy in Spain. Ingres depicted Lucien, a poet, connoisseur and archaeologist, who had been barred from high office by an unpopular marriage, sitting on a marble relief, looking up from his book with a view of the Quirinal behind. The carefully pencilled style suggests a date of 1807–08.

(above right)
15 *Portrait of Madame Guillon-Lethière and Her Son*
NEW YORK, Metropolitan Museum of Art (Mrs. H. O. Havemeyer bequest). Pencil on paper 24·1 × 18·7 cm. Signed: Ingres, Rome 1808.

Guillaume Guillon-Lethière's career as a painter was spanned by two vast canvases, *Virginia* and *Brutus*. In between these works he was artistic adviser to Lucien Bonaparte in Spain and succeeded Suvée as director of the Ecole de Rome in 1807. Ingres was closely associated with his family until Guillon-Lethière was removed from his post at the fall of the Empire. Guillon-Lethière opened a studio on his return to Paris, where he died in 1832. Ingres drew this portrait of Mme. Guillon-Lethière with her illegitimate son by Lucien Bonaparte not long after her family had arrived at the Villa Medici, where Suvée had re-established the Ecole de Rome. The villa figures appropriately in the background, with the towers of the Trinità dei Monte on the right, drawn with the sharp, pencilled outline characteristic of the setting of many of Ingres's Roman portraits.

(opposite)
16 *Oedipus and the Sphinx*
PARIS, Musée du Louvre. Oil on canvas 189 × 144 cm. Signed: I. Ingres Pingebat 1808.

Included among the works sent by Ingres to the Académie in Paris in 1808, as a nude study, this composition was enlarged in the 1820s by Ingres, who then, as a Poussinesque touch, added the man turning away in terror in order to accentuate the drama of the two figures. The sphinx's paw raised to strike, the scattered bones of victims and the Romantic chasm give relief to Oedipus's quiet courage as he answers the riddle. His pose is an Antique commonplace. The features have been recast in the Davidian ideal, although Ingres angrily denied that he had idealized the model who posed in Rome for Oedipus. 'I only copy nature and never idealize.'

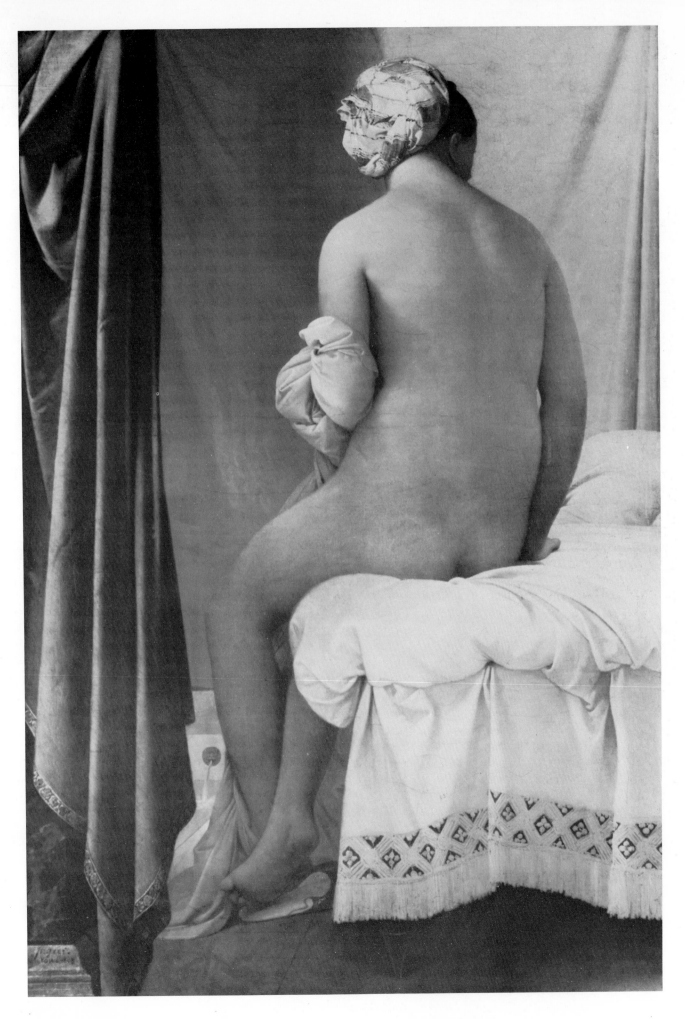

(*page* 32)
17 *The Bathing Woman*

BAYONNE, Musée Bonnat. Oil on canvas mounted on panel 51 × 42 cm. Signed: Ingres Pinxit Roma 1807.

This small, half-length study, the first in a long series of female nudes, was possibly connected with the nude academic studies which students at the Ecole de Rome were obliged to paint. The twist of the model's head and the long curve of her back as she turns, surprised, at the water's edge, make an elegant effect. Amaury-Duval, seeing the panel in Ingres's studio in 1825, was struck by the difference between this study and his prize-winning *Ambassadors of Agamemnon*: 'that is because I still had not seen Italy,' said Ingres, 'when I did this picture, and this study is the first I painted under the inspiration of the masters.' The smooth, opaque paint without glazing or scumbling and the small Peruginesque features show the influence of his Italian studies.

(*page* 33)
18 *The Valpinçon Bather*

PARIS, Musée du Louvre. Oil on canvas 146 × 97·5 cm. Signed: Ingres, Rome 1808.

Among the works which Ingres sent to the Paris Académie in 1808 was this back view of a seated bather. The idea is linked to the earlier bather (Plate 17) and raises the possibility that *The Bathing Woman* was originally intended as a full-length painting. The works were not unfavourably received, but Ingres was criticized for not giving enough value to the effect of light and was asked to take note of the best masters of the Roman School. Ingres, however, was already in full flight from the conventions of chiaroscuro inherited from sixteenth-century Roman art which he had mastered in Paris. The shadows of *The Valpinçon Bather*, so called after one of its owners, were painted with opaque colour which destroys the rich contrasts of academic chiaroscuro and substitutes Ingres's own, subtly modelled effect of light which has been compared, justly, to Vermeer.

(*opposite*)
III *The Dream of Ossian*

MONTAUBAN, Musée Ingres. Oil on canvas 348 × 275 cm. Signed: Ingres F. 1813.

Napoleon I had a particular fondness for Macpherson's forged verses, purporting to have been composed by Ossian, northern Europe's answer to Homer, and more in keeping with the age of sensibility than the violence of his Greek counterpart. This composition was commissioned for the emperor's bedroom in the Quirinal Palace in 1811, as the work by Gérard, which inspired it, had been commissioned for Josephine's Malmaison. Ossian, old and lonely, asleep in a rocky, moonlit landscape, dreams of the heroes, including his own dead son, and the heroines whose exploits he had celebrated in his epics. The theme connects with *Virgil Reading the 'Aeneid'* which probably also originated as a commission for the Quirinal, but whereas the composition of *Virgil*, like the subject, is conventionally classical, Ingres's harp-playing choir at the centre of *Ossian* is taken from the angels who close the composition in many early Renaissance altarpieces. In the parlance of 1811, this vaporous nocturne, like the works of Chateaubriand and Girodet is *romantique*. Ossian ranked with Homer, Oedipus and Belisarius as one of the archetypal outcasts in European Neo-Classical art, a hero of the cult of suffering which was a feature of the period. In 1835 Ingres succeeded in repurchasing this ceiling painting and began to transform it, with the help of his pupil Raymond Balze, not from an oval to a square, as is generally thought, but, according to Mlle. Toussaint's plausible theory, from a square to an oval. Whatever the fact of the matter, the work was eventually left in suspension between an oval and a square, marred in some respects by the pupil's dead overpainting.

(*above left*)
19 *Portrait of Edme Bochet*
PARIS, Musée du Louvre. Oil on canvas 94×69 cm. Signed: Ingres, Roma 1811.

Edme Bochet, an official in the government of Rome during the French occupation, introduced his relation Marcotte to Ingres's fellow student, Gatteaux, at the Académie. Gatteaux in turn put the Marcotte family in touch with Ingres and, shortly after completing the portrait of Marcotte (Plate 21), Ingres painted this portrait of Bochet.

(*above right*)
20 *Portrait of Mme. Panckoucke*
PARIS, Musée du Louvre. Oil on canvas 93×68 cm. Signed: J. Ingres, Rome, 1811.

Through Bochet, Ingres received a further commission for a portrait of his sister, Mme. Panckoucke. Her pose, which complements her brother's (Plate 19) and which was probably intended for an oval frame, loses its formal *raison d'être* in its present four-sided state and has, thus, acquired a mannered appearance.

(*opposite*)
IV *Portrait of Madame Leblanc*
NEW YORK, Metropolitan Museum of Art (Wolfe fund). Oil on canvas 119·4×92·7 cm. Signed: Ingres P. flor. 1823.

Visiting Florence in 1820, Ingres met the family of a Swiss businessman who put him in touch with several patrons, including a Frenchman, Jacques-Louis Leblanc, living in Florence on a fortune made in occupied Italy. Ingres executed half a dozen portrait drawings of the Leblanc family and a pair of oil portraits of Leblanc and his wife. In the portrait of Leblanc, also in the Metropolitan, the sitter looks up from his book with a genial smile in a pose complementing that of his wife, who sits back in her chair, as Robert Rosenblum points out, like David's *Mme. de Verinac* or Canova's *Madame Mère*. In either case, her relaxed pose links her with the informal naturalism of David's portrait style. Her black dress, unadorned apart from her chatelaine and long gold chain, confirms the Biedermeier sobriety of her ambience. The dull orange of her shawl picks up the tones of polished wood against the dark background. Her complaisant features have no airs, but the grace of her pale complexion and elongated neck, worthy of Lawrence, is echoed by the pink rose on the marble table, bringing a note of tenderness into this comfortable Florentine ménage.

21 *Portrait of Charles Marcotte d'Argenteuil*
WASHINGTON, National Gallery of Art (Samuel H. Kress collection). Oil on canvas 93·5 × 69·3 cm.
Signed: Ingres pinx. Rome 1810.

Charles Marcotte, sent by Napoleon to Rome in 1810 to set up a board for controlling the forests
in the Roman States, was advised by the engraver Edouard Gatteaux to commission his portrait
from Ingres. This solid, soberly coloured painting, lacking the characteristic panache of Ingres's
portraits, began a lifelong friendship between Marcotte and Ingres which ended with Marcotte's
death in 1864 at the age of ninety.

22 *Portrait of Joseph Antoine Moltedo*
NEW YORK, Metropolitan Museum of Art (Mrs. H. O. Havemeyer bequest). 1810. Oil on canvas
75·3 × 58·1 cm. Unsigned.

This portrait of the French director of posts in the Roman States, whose activities ranged widely in
government and commerce during the occupation, makes effective use of the subject's heavy bulk
and square head. The Colosseum in the background is appropriately massive in a recessed landscape
which Moltedo's hat and collar nearly exclude. The composition is built up on solid squares,
giving an effect of stability to the sitter's character, and he is viewed almost symmetrically from
the front, with only a slight bias to one side adding movement and interest to the pose.

23 *Portrait of Jacques Marquet de Montbreton de Norvins*
LONDON, National Gallery. Oil on canvas 97 × 79 cm. Signed: Ingres P. Ro.

It is not difficult to imagine the baron de Norvins as the shrewd, ruthless head of police in occupied Rome. A bust of the goddess Athena, representing Rome, is placed in the background, no doubt drawing attention delicately to the wisdom of the French rule. The strong contrast of red and black reinforces the bluntness of Norvin's character. Ingres seems to have worked on the portrait from 1811 to 1813, and there are conspicuous, untypical pentimenti visible around the head, on the costume and on the pedestal of the bust.

24 *Portrait of the comtesse de Tournon*
PHILADELPHIA, collection of Henry P. McIlhenny. Oil on canvas 93 × 73 cm. Signed: Ingres Rome 1812.

Although this is Ingres's only painted portrait of an elderly woman there are a number of drawings which share with this portrait an acuity of vision and sense of character which were sometimes blurred by younger charms. The model was mother of the prefect of the Tiber region and belonged to the colony of Ingres's patrons in occupied Rome.

25 *The Family of Lucien Bonaparte*
CAMBRIDGE (MASSACHUSETTS), Fogg Art Museum (Grenville L. Winthrop bequest). Pencil on paper
41·2 × 52·9 cm. Signed: J. Ingres Del. Rome 1815.

Towards the end of the Empire Ingres undertook two large family portraits of the Napoleonic
dynasties in Italy, the abandoned portrait of Murat's family and this large drawing of Lucien
Bonaparte's family showing Lucien's second wife with his children by both marriages. Lucien
himself is represented only by a bust in the space he might have occupied had he not been absent
during the Hundred Days supporting the cause of his brother at Waterloo. Like *The Stamaty Family*
(Plate 27), this drawing represents the *Mater Familias* presiding over the accomplishments and
amusements of her children.

(*opposite*)
26 *Portrait of Madame de Senonnes*
NANTES, Musée des Beaux-Arts. 1814–16. Oil on canvas 106 × 84 cm. Signed: Ing. Roma.

The small head with vapid features seems out of scale with the splendour of the costume. Like the
idealization of form in Ingres's portraits, the idealization of colour accentuates the sense of
character. The scarlet velvet dress with shining satin in the slashes, boldly juxtaposed to the
mound of gold cushions, gives the sitter the airs of an odalisque. Ingres at first considered the
reclining pose which he gave to *The Grande Odalisque* (Plate 34), but decided finally for a more
upright one, the sitter facing the spectator. For the first time in a portrait, Ingres used the device
of a mirror to give depth and contrast in a picture of shallow recession and bright colours.

(*above left*)
27 *The Stamaty Family*
PARIS, Musée du Louvre, Cabinet des Dessins. Pencil on paper 46 × 37 cm. Signed: J. A. Ingres Del. roma 1818.

Constantin Stamaty, supporter of the French Revolution and leader of a movement dedicated to Greek rebellion, married Marie-Thérèse-Nanine Surdan illegally before a priest in 1798, influenced by his fiancée's strong Catholic beliefs. In Ingres's drawing, the former revolutionary, now vice-consul in Civitavecchia and an amiable father, stands behind his accomplished family; his wife, an excellent musician, represents, as H. Naef remarks, 'the moral centre of the family'. Their daughter, Atala, whose godfather was Chateaubriand, fingers the square piano. She was an amateur artist. Camille, leaning on his mother's knee, became a professional composer and pianist, and Joachim-Emmanuel, standing behind his mother's chair, became a geographical engineer. On the wall, Ingres placed a version of the head and shoulders of his *Grande Odalisque*, resembling a small canvas in the Louvre, which repeats the turn of Atala's head. Both Atala, whose head is more carefully worked than the others, and the odalisque share the languid charm of Ingres's ideal.

(*above right*)
28 *Portrait of Madame Destouches*
PARIS, Musée du Louvre, Cabinet des Dessins. Pencil on paper 43 × 28.5 cm. Signed: Ingres Delineavi[t] rome 1816.

Armande Destouches arrived in Rome with her husband Louis, a winner of the Prix de Rome in architecture, in 1816. Previously, she had been married to his brother, an officer who died on campaign in 1813 after making Louis promise to propose to Armande. Ingres drew her portrait with the freedom of pencil typical of his portrait-drawings at this date, stopping with care over the features of the face, framed in sharply sculpted curls. With his characteristic tyranny for the sake of detail, he made her turn her hat back to front so the ostrich feathers contain her head inside the oval movement of the composition and add a touch of caprice to her novelettish charms. Writing to her father in Paris in December 1816 she described her portrait 'drawn by a famous artist, M. Ingres, who, by the way, has so flattered me that he has almost turned me into a pretty woman'.

(*opposite*)
29 *Jupiter and Thetis*
AIX-EN-PROVENCE, Musée Granet. Oil on canvas 327 × 260 cm. Signed: Ingres. Rome. 1811.

In the last year of their scholarship art students at the French Ecole de Rome were expected to send to Paris a historic composition of their choice. Ingres's work, inspired by the episode in the *Iliad* in which Thetis implores Jupiter's intervention in the Trojan wars on the side of her son, Achilles, and meditated since 1806, was severely criticized by the judges in Paris. Ingres was accused again of wilful regression to Gothic art because of the flatness of the colours and the insufficient modelling of the figures. His sources were a patchwork of derivations from Girodet

and Flaxman (Thetis), from Greek statuary (Jupiter) and from an Antique cameo (the base of the throne). The exaggerations, however, are not to be judged by standards of realism but by their powers of expression. The intensely brooding face of Jupiter, leaning on the storm clouds, the pliant, anxious Thetis, tiny by comparison, and Juno's jealous face merging into the clouds, are intensely felt aspects of a situation charged with contrasting emotions and a passionate response to physical beauty.

30 *Romulus, Victor over Acron, Carries the Spoils of War to the Temple of Jupiter*
PARIS, Musée du Louvre, Cabinet des Dessins. Pencil and ink wash with added white on paper
34 × 53 cm. Signed: J. Ingres in. Pit Roma 1808.

In 1812 the Palace of the Quirinal in Rome was redecorated as a residence for Napoleon. Ingres
with other artists received commissions to supply decorative panels. *Romulus* was intended for a
room dedicated to the battles of Antiquity and illustrates an episode in Plutarch's life of Romulus,
no doubt delicately justifying the Napoleonic habit of organizing pillage for the benefit of the
Louvre. Ingres's composition blends appropriate borrowings from the horses of the Quirinal with a
more general debt to David's *Battle of the Sabines* and Mantegna's *Triumph of Caesar* at Hampton
Court. The pale matt tonality, imitating fresco, was determined by the decorative nature of the
project. The whole ensemble was dismantled by Pope Pius VII in 1815 on the withdrawal of the
French from Rome. This drawing is clearly much later than the painting and shows the
characteristic variants in a number of the figures which might trap the unwary into supposing it to
be a preparatory study. Professor Ternois has suggested that it may have been drawn for the
engraving by Reveil of 1851. The error in the date, which refers to the original painting and not to
the drawing, is also characteristic of Ingres's habit of antedating his work and should not be seen
as evidence that Ingres had the composition in mind four years before he received the commission.

31 *The Death of Leonardo*
PARIS, Petit Palais. Oil on canvas 40 × 50·5 cm. Signed: Ingres Pinxit 1818.

Like *Henri IV Receiving the Spanish Ambassador* (Plate 37), *The Death of Leonardo* was painted for Blacas and was exhibited at the Salon of 1824. The episode of Leonardo dying in the arms of François I, taken from Vasari and very flattering to the artistic career, anticipates the subject of Molière at the table of Louis XIV, which Ingres painted in 1857 (Paris, Comédie Française), showing the same contrast between the attentions of the monarch to an artist and the disfavour of the court. Leonardo's pupil at the end of the bed throws his arms out in a gesture of appeal to the stony onlookers which was borrowed from his master's *Last Supper* and which, perhaps, invites them to see the image of Christ in the dying artist.

32 *Cardinal Bibiena Offering his Niece to Raphael in Marriage* or *The Betrothal of Raphael*
BALTIMORE, Walters Art Gallery. c. 1813. Oil on paper mounted on panel 59 × 46 cm. Signed:
Ingres.

Like many of his colleagues in the nineteenth century, Ingres was attracted to the lives of the
artists as a source of wishful thinking. He was especially drawn to episodes showing, often with
little historic basis, the acknowledged superiority of artists in the past; Raphael receives
his fiancée from the hand of the cardinal as Apelles received his mistress from the hand of
Alexander. Similarly, Leonardo dies in the arms of the King of France, and Tintoretto asserts
superiority over Aretino. The heads of the three main characters in this picture were taken from
sources in the work of Raphael and his circle. The myth, in Ingres's own case, became a reality as
he was intimate with the Orléans family and with the Imperial family which succeeded them, and
as his second wife came from the family of his patron, Marcotte.

(opposite)
33 *Raphael and the Fornarina*
CAMBRIDGE (MASSACHUSETTS), Fogg Art Museum (Grenville L. Winthrop bequest). Oil on canvas
68 × 55 cm. Signed: Ingres, Roma.

Painted for the comte de Pourtalès in 1814, this picture is probably close to a first version of the

subject lost in Riga during the invasion of 1941. Ingres, who had broken off his first engagement for the sake of his career, seems to describe in this composition a relationship between life and art as Raphael turns from the attentions of his mistress to contemplate his art. On the easel is the so-called *Fornarina* in the Galleria Nazionale in Rome, then attributed to Raphael. The view of a Renaissance palazzo through the window recalls Raphael's achievement as an architect, while the ubiquitous *Madonna della Sedia* represents his genius in painting. The features of Raphael's mistress and her pose were, significantly, not based on the portrait in Rome but on the *Madonna della Sedia*, stressing the Fornarina, endowed with the attributes of Raphael's Virgin, in her rôle as the artist's muse. This point was made more precisely in three other versions of the same composition in which the Fornarina leans over Raphael in an exact imitation of the Madonna clasping the Christ child in her arms. Raphael's features were based on the portrait of Bindo Altoviti in Washington, then thought to be a self-portrait of Raphael.

34 *The Grande Odalisque*
PARIS, Musée du Louvre. Oil on canvas 91 × 162 cm. Signed: I. A. Ingres P.AT 1814 Rom.

The subject of *The Grande Odalisque* belongs to the world of Mozart's *Entführung aus dem Serail*.
She is the play-acting nude of Boucher's *Odalisque* in the Louvre turned into the type of
Ingres's langorous ideal. Fantasy invades the style. Painted for Caroline Murat as a pendant
to the lost *Sleeping Woman*, but never delivered owing to the fall of the Empire, *The Grande
Odalisque* was sent by Ingres to the Salon of 1819, where the distended anatomy and lack of
traditional modelling bewildered the critics. Her pose recalls David's *Madame Récamier*, which had

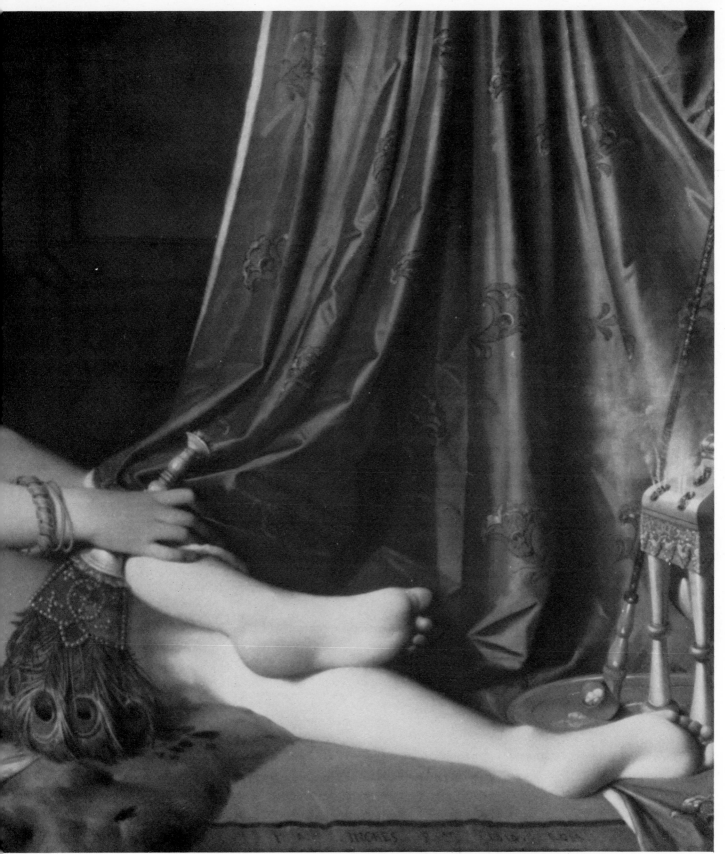

been painted with some assistance from the young Ingres, while her head was based upon Raphael's *Madonna della Sedia*, strangely transformed as in a dream. The luxurious texture of silk, fur, jewellery and feathers add to the tactile sensuousness of the composition. The oranges and browns with touches of scarlet in the details resonate with the near monochrome of flesh. The arabesque of form and thin, flat paint, reducing the evidence of the brushwork, gave Ingres the reputation of being an artist in outlines and a dead colourist, but every inch of *The Grande Odalisque* is alive with the movement of his brush, flowing thinly over the finely grained canvas with astonishing accuracy, blurring the outlines of the flesh for an effect of softness and touching in details with a spirited stroke.

35 *The Interior of the Sistine Chapel*
WASHINGTON, National Gallery of Art (Samuel H. Kress collection). Oil on canvas 74·5 × 92·7 cm.
Signed: Ingres 181[4] rom.

During Holy Week 1807 Ingres was moved to tears by the music of the Sistine Chapel heard
under the 'awesome picture of the Last Judgement whose prodigious effect impresses a sort of terror
in the soul'. Ingres painted or projected a number of ceremonial interiors of a type associated with
Granet, who was at the height of his popularity during the Restoration. The presentation of *The
Sistine Chapel*, however, is not like Granet's Gothic vaults, for Ingres's interior, with the foreground
figures cut in half for visibility in a manner which is not common in early nineteenth-century art,
recalls instead Italian sixteenth-century illustrations of similar occasions. Professor Ternois posits a
derivation from a picture by Agostino Tasso (1580–1644), whose dry reportage would not have
allowed Ingres scope for the expression of emotion, but *The Last Judgement* makes a solemn contrast
with the richly decorated walls, recalling Ingres's response to the pomp and drama of the setting. In
order not to sacrifice a telling point Ingres flattened out the corner of the Sistine Chapel, giving an
effect of collage to *The Last Judgement* and upsetting the perspective of the canopy. As Pope Pius
VII was then in exile, Ingres hesitated, for political reasons, to include him, but Marcotte, who
commissioned the work, encouraged him to include the pope, who occupies the centre of the
composition, improperly robed for the occasion in white and gold to give prominence to his person.
The portraits of those in attendance, including a self-portrait, were drawn from memory.

(*opposite*)
V *The Odalisque with the Slave*
BALTIMORE, Walters Art Gallery. Oil on canvas 76 × 105 cm. Signed: J. Ingres 1842.

This replica of the composition of 1839 (Plate 52) was painted for William I, King of
Württemberg. Ingres changed the bold shapes on the carpet in the original for a more discreet
pattern of green foliage. The landscape in the background was added by Ingres's pupil, Paul
Flandrin. Ingres was rarely so well served by the collaboration of a pupil. The dancing figure in
the garden was derived from a set of costume prints which Ingres owned and had already used as
a source for the *Interior of a Harem* (Paris, Musée du Louvre) in 1828.

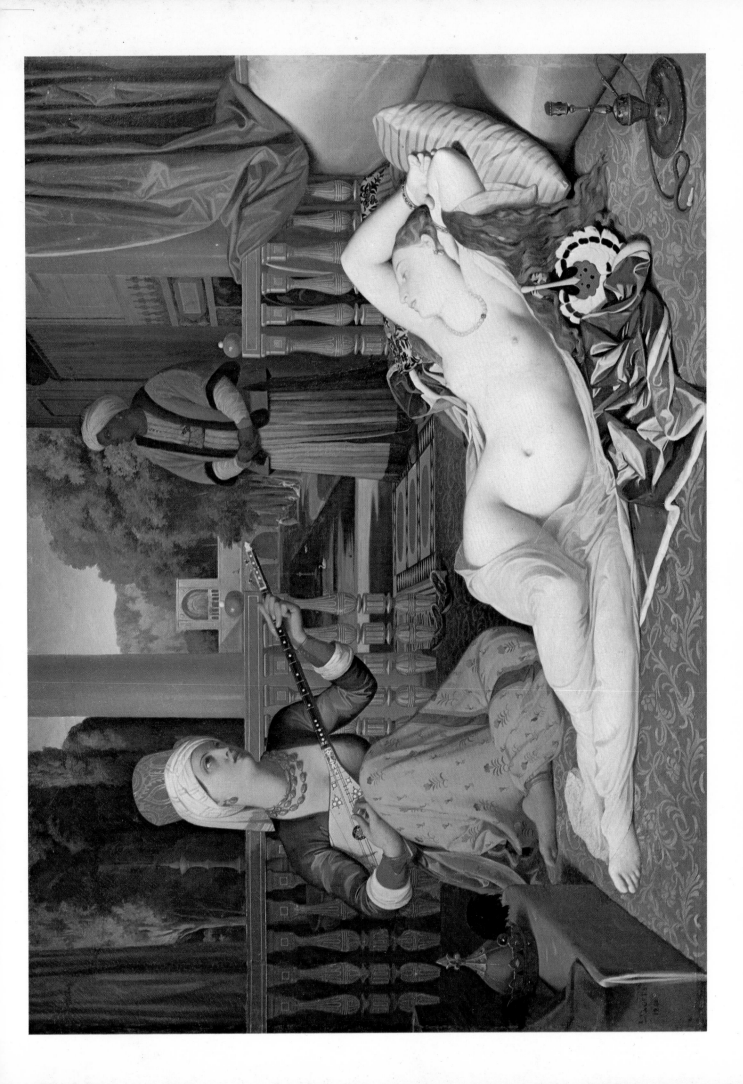

36　*The Entry of the Dauphin, later Charles V, into Paris*
HARTFORD, Wadsworth Atheneum. Oil on panel 47 × 56 cm. Signed: J. Ingres 1821.

In 1358 Jean Pastourel with his fellow regents arranged the return of the dauphin to Paris after the disturbances led by Etienne Marcel had been suppressed. Of all the historic genre pictures commissioned from Ingres, none shows the importance of politics so clearly as this panel, commissioned in Florence by the marquis de Pastoret, whose alleged descent from Jean Pastourel encouraged this reference to his own loyalty to the restored Bourbon monarchy. Guided by Pastoret, Ingres followed closely the account given in Froissart's chronicle. The main details are all taken, as Hans Naef has discovered, from Montfaucon's *Monuments de la monarchie française*, which accounts for the evident affinity with manuscript illustrations. By 1824, however, Ingres was in full flight from those 'little monsters', as he called his pictures of historic genre.

(opposite)
VI *Portrait of the vicomtesse d'Haussonville*
NEW YORK, Frick Collection. Oil on canvas 131·8 × 92 cm. Signed: Ingres 1845.

Because Ingres resented his reputation as a painter of portraits, he refused many commissions after his retreat to Rome in 1834. On his return to Paris in 1841, he was not always able to resist friendly pressure or the charm of the model. In 1842 he agreed to paint the portrait of the vicomtesse d'Haussonville, 'our pretty little savage viscountess' as Ingres called her. By June he had sketched her portrait on the canvas placing her leaning forward on a chair in the pose of Stratonice. A year later, he began the picture again, retaining the reflective pose but placing her against a mantelpiece decorated in blue with a pair of ormolu-mounted vases and two jardinières in *bleu de saxe*. Her pale blue dress stands out against the detail of the background and her head is given depth and contrast by the overmantel glass. A new casual element appears in the composition in the less artful placing of furniture and drapery than in previous portraits and in the diagonal recession, which, distancing the vicomtesse d'Haussonville from her reflection, gives a feeling of space beyond the picture edge.

37 *Henri IV Receiving the Spanish Ambassador*
PARIS, Petit Palais. Oil on canvas 39 × 49 cm. Signed: Ingres Pinxit Roma 1817.

In 1817 the comte de Blacas, the French ambassador in Rome, commissioned this image of the popular monarchy, thus underlining his own ultra-royalist sympathies. Ingres shared his nation's passion for Henri IV, and Lapauze counted fifteen different episodes from the life of the first Bourbon king in the artist's notes listed for future reference. The subject comes from a life of Henri by Péréfixe, who recounted how the Spanish ambassador found the king playing with his family. The composition, however, derives from a painting by Revoil, a colleague and friend of Ingres at David's studio. Revoil's picture was exhibited at the Salon of 1817 while Ingres was absent in Italy, but he would certainly have known it from a contemporary line engraving in Landon's *Annales*. Ingres's friends, Granet, Bergeret and Richard, had pioneered interest in Henri IV in the Salons of the First Empire. Napoleon admired his Bourbon predecessor, but understandably, enthusiasm for Henri IV was at its maximum in the Restoration. The numbers of scenes from the life of this king chart the profile of the fashion; the total for successive Salons is given in brackets: 1804–1812 (15); 1814 (20); 1817 (16); 1819 (19); 1822 (14); 1824 (21); 1827 (8); 1831 (8); 1833 (2); 1834 (2); 1835 (1). Ingres exhibited *Henri IV Receiving the Spanish Ambassador* at the height of the vogue in 1824, and his loss of interest in historic genre in the mid 1820s paralleled a general decline of enthusiasm for Medieval and Renaissance history during the same period. Raphael's *Madonna della Sedia* appears, again, on the wall.

56

38 *Don Pedro de Toledo Kissing the Sword of Henri IV*
OSLO, private collection. Oil on panel 48 × 40 cm. Signed: J. Ingres Pinx. Roma 1820.

This panel repeats the composition of a lost work of the same subject exhibited without much
success at the Salon of 1814 and now known only from a line engraving. Marcotte himself had
reservations. 'I could', answered Ingres, 'have given more distance to the background, but many
pictures err in this respect, particularly those of the Italian School.' As in a number of his works,
The Death of Leonardo for instance, the episode was originally set inside a structure of verticals and
horizontals with only slight recession, recalling Ingres's debt to the formal geometry of the Neo-
Classical. Comparison between this version in Oslo and the engraving of the lost original shows that
Ingres took the criticism to heart. He stressed in a letter to Gilibert in 1822, in case he heard any
criticism of the previous work, that the background of this picture had been totally revised. Ingres
tilted the composition, turning the ambassador inward so his leg forms a diagonal and showing
the room in the Louvre with the caryatids of Jean Goujon in steep perspective. However, the
monumental appearance of the architecture now conflicts with the elegant foreground pair whose
pose was originally devised for a wholly different, more classical treatment of the setting. The
episode is taken from Péréfixe's life of Henri IV. Don Pedro, the Spanish ambassador, meeting a
page with the king's sword, kneels to kiss 'the most glorious sword in Christendom'. Ingres designed
the frame himself, basing it upon the inset picture of Marie de' Medici in Rubens's *Presentation of
the Portrait*, plain, black wood with no ornament or gilding of any kind.

39 *Roger Freeing Angelica*
PARIS, Musée du Louvre. Oil on canvas 147 × 199 cm. Signed: J. A. D. Ingres, P.it Roma 1819.

Roger Freeing Angelica was prominently exhibited at the Salon of 1819 and bought for 2000 francs
for Louis XVIII's collection at the suggestion of Blacas. The high favour enjoyed by Ingres
contrasted with the hostility of critics. As the picture appeared only in the supplement to the
catalogue (presumably it was submitted late), a number of critics failed to identify the subject
which illustrates Roger rescuing Angelica from the orc in Book X of Ariosto's *Orlando Furioso*, a
long-established source of Romantic inspiration for French artists. The blend of sharp realism and
fantasy in the figure of Roger mounted on his hippogriff, attacking the orc with his lance, evokes
the atmosphere of Ariosto's mock heroic tale. Ingres, at first, thought of showing Angelica overcome
with shame, incapable of concealing her face with her hands on account of her chains (lines
685–694), but finally invented a pose which expresses the violence of conflicting emotions. Roger,
bearing his magic shield, prods the monster's tusks, which Ingres, following Ariosto, copied from a
boar. 'On the whole', said P. A. Coupin, a critic more sensitive than most to the virtues of Ingres,
'this picture is well worth considering but is little considered, and then only by artists.' Robert
Lefèvre exhibited the same subject in 1822, and Delacroix, seeing Ingres's version in the
Luxembourg in 1824, found it charming.

(*opposite*)
40 *Paolo and Francesca*
ANGERS, Musée des Beaux-Arts. Oil on canvas 48 × 39 cm. Signed: Ingres, Rom. 1819.

A first, smaller version of this picture, painted for Caroline Murat, is now in the Musée Condé,
Chantilly. This second version, commissioned by the Société des Amis des Arts in Paris, is set in a
box-like interior derived, according to Naef, from a fresco attributed to Masolino in the church of
San Clemente in Rome. The general lines of the composition were taken from a painting
exhibited at the Salon of 1812 by Coupin de la Couperie, an artist friend of Ingres. The figure of
Paolo is derived from Raphael's *Mass of Bolsena*; his elongated neck gives emphasis to his passionate
lunge at Francesca, who drops her book in the emotion. The tragic love of Paolo for Francesca,
wife of his brother Gianciotto da Rimini, as told by Dante in Book V of *The Inferno*, became a
favourite theme of French Romantic art. Reading together an account of the love of Sir Lancelot
for Queen Guinevere, they reached the point where Lancelot embraced the queen. Paolo
interrupted their reading with a kiss as the jealous Gianciotto entered and killed the pair with his
sword. The picture was rejected by the Société des Amis des Arts and acquired by one of its
members, the amateur artist Turpin de Crissé. The contemporary Gothic frame, matching the
colours of the composition, might have been designed by Ingres, who took extreme care to suit the
frames to his pictures.

(above left)
41   *Portrait of Niccolò Paganini*
PARIS, Musée du Louvre, Cabinet des Dessins. Pencil on paper 29·8 × 21·8 cm. Signed: Ingres
Del. roma 1819.

A skilful violinist himself, Ingres enjoyed the company of musicians. At the time of his first stay in
Rome he played second violin in quartets organized by Paganini, whose own playing was admired
by Ingres at this period. Between Ingres's departure from Italy in 1824 and Paganini's visit to
France in 1831, the Italian had acquired his reputation as a virtuoso of diabolical bravura. Ingres,
who disliked virtuosity, was deeply chagrined by the change in his friend's technique. Unlike
Delacroix's sketch of Paganini in the Louvre (fig. 4, p. 11), which vibrates with the intensity of the
performance, Ingres's drawing, dating from the years in Rome, shows Paganini smiling blandly at
the artist, carrying his violin like an attribute of his profession.

(above right)
42   *Portrait of Lorenzo Bartolini*
PARIS, Musée du Louvre. Oil on canvas 108 × 85·7 cm. Signed: Bartolini statuaire, peint par
Ingres à Florence 1820.

Ingres met the sculptor Bartolini at David's studio. The two men then shared a studio at the
Capuchin convent where, with Bergeret, a historic genre painter, they made a speciality of studying
the art of the Italian Renaissance. In 1806, Ingres had painted a dark, Byronic portrait of Bartolini,
hardly recognizable as the prosperous sculptor of this later portrait. On the table lies the evidence
of the interests they shared, a bust of Cherubini, a partita by Haydn, works by Dante, Homer and
Machiavelli. Ingres lived for a time with Bartolini after leaving Rome in 1820, tempted by the
prospects of patronage in Florence of which the sculptor had a rich share, but Florence was not as
promising as it had appeared. Mme. Ingres seems to have disliked Bartolini, and Ingres himself
eventually quarrelled with his old colleague.

(opposite)
43   *Portrait of Madame Marcotte de Sainte-Marie*
PARIS, Musée du Louvre. Oil on canvas 93 × 74 cm. Signed: Ingres 1826.

In this portrait of his patron's sister-in-law, Ingres returned to the reclining pose which he had used
for *Madame de Senonnes* (Plate 26) but to such different effect that the kinship is not immediately
obvious. Whereas everything in *Madame de Senonnes* is bright and strident the portrait of Mme. de
Marcotte, with its predominance of brown and gold, is gentle and muted. Holding her lorgnette
aside for an instant, Mme. de Marcotte looks up with a quizzical look in her extraordinary eyes,
which draw the spectator's attention, while Mme. de Senonnes's vacuous face fails to compete with
the splendour of her accessories.

44 *Portrait of the Count Gouriev*
LENINGRAD, Hermitage Museum. Oil on canvas 107 × 86 cm. Signed: Ingres Flor. 1821.

Professor Ternois has established that the model, a Russian officer in the wars against Napoleon
and later ambassador at The Hague, was in Florence in 1821 on his honeymoon. The formula used
in the portraits of Granet, Moltedo and Cordier, was here given a new authority by emphasizing
the tall, slender form of Gouriev, whose eye level is above that of the spectator. The effect is partly
achieved by the nearly square shape of the canvas, giving a new sense of space around the model.
The background clouds touched with the last red of evening above the blue, smoking hills and the
woods, already absorbed by shadow, contrast with the spare elegance of the count wrapped
against the chill in his black, scarlet lined cloak. Many of Ingres's models carry an article in hand,
often a hat, like a badge of office, and Ingres gave to Gouriev the glove, clasped in a gloved hand,
the traditional attribute of the gentleman and aristocrat in portraiture.

(opposite)
45 *Portrait of Amédée-David de Pastoret*
CHICAGO, Art Institute of Chicago. Oil on canvas 100 × 82 cm. Signed: Ingres 1826.

The model, after a brilliant diplomatic career under Napoleon, wisely remained aloof during the

Hundred Days and began a new career devoted to the Bourbons. The nobility of his family, which was of very recent date, was captured by Ingres in this portrait by using the formula devised for the portrait of Gouriev; the tall, spare figure rises into the ample space of the canvas and looks slightly down at the spectator. He does not hold his yellow gloves but they are there nevertheless. Ingres wrote to Pastoret, reminding him to bring these essential items to the sitting. The gloves give a slight frisson of bright colour to the blacks and greens which predominate. The black embroidery on a black ground on his costume strikes a note of quiet elegance without distracting from the head. 'What if the costume had been embroidered with green or blue palm branches like some official costumes . . . ?' asked Amaury-Duval. 'I would not have done it' replied Ingres.

46 *Christ Giving the Keys of Heaven to St. Peter*
MONTAUBAN, Musée Ingres. Oil on canvas 280 × 217 cm.
Signed: J. Ingres Rom. 1820.

Trained as a history painter, Ingres resented the lack of
opportunity between 1812 and 1817 to work on a large
important commission. The director of the Ecole de
Rome, knowing that Ingres was anxious to exercise his
talent as a history painter, persuaded Blacas in 1817 to
commission *Christ Giving the Keys to St. Peter* for the
French convent attached to S. Trinità. The painted
sketch was ready by 1818 and the work completed by the
summer of 1820 when it was seen and admired,
according to Ingres, by 'friends and enemies alike'.
Ingres combined studies of beauty and naturalism in the
heads of St. Peter and St. Matthew with a general debt
to Raphael's cartoon, now in London, of *Feed My
Sheep*. Ingres's imagination reveals itself in the movement
of the draperies which fuse Christ and St. Peter into a
single emphasis thrusting upwards from the rock on
which they are standing towards heaven.

(*opposite*)
47 *The Vow of Louis XIII*
MONTAUBAN, Cathedral of Notre-Dame. Oil on canvas 421 × 262 cm. Signed: J. Ingres 1824;
inscribed: VIRG. DEIP. REGN. VOV LUDOV. XIII A.R.S.H. MDCXXXVIII FEB.

In 1820 Ingres received a commission, prompted by his childhood friend, Gilibert, from the
Minister of the Interior for a painting for the cathedral at Montauban. The mayor and the
cathedral chapter decided that the subject was to be Louis XIII dedicating France to the Virgin
on the Feast of the Assumption in 1638. Ingres misunderstood the brief note he received with details
of the subject to mean that he was expected to paint Louis XIII and his courtiers present at the
Assumption of the Virgin. Ingres insisted that such a programme was an impossible anachronism,
but before receiving a letter explaining the misunderstanding, he devised a way of treating the
subject with propriety by assuming that the king, on the day of his vow, saw a vision of the
Assumption. Eventually, he abandoned the idea of the Assumption altogether and painted
something like the vision of St. Luke, borrowing a variety of motifs from Raphael for the occasion.
Ingres's letters show the pains he took to document the appearance of the king, using as his main
source for the costume a portrait by Pourbus of Henri IV in the Uffizi. In 1824 Ingres accompanied
the completed work to Paris, where it had an outstanding success at the Salon. The Raphaelesque
element seemed well contained by its subject, and Ingres returning to Paris like an artist from the
past seemed to offer a promising way out of the disorders of Romanticism and the decadence of
Classicism.

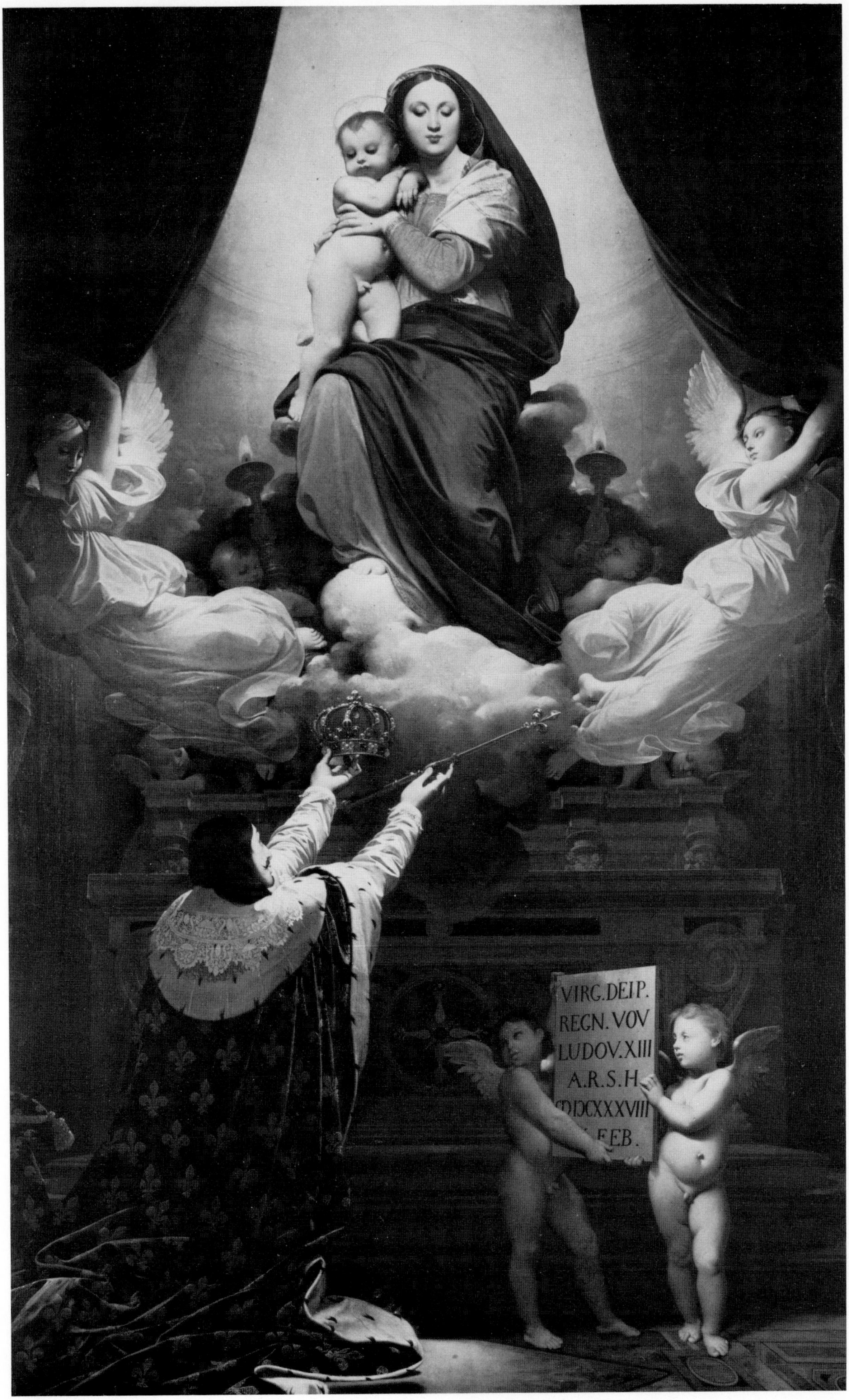
VIRG.DEIP.
REGN.VOV
LUDOV.XIII
A.R.S.H
FEB.

48 *The Apotheosis of Homer*

PARIS, Musée du Louvre. Oil on canvas 386 × 515 cm. Signed: INGRES PING^{ba} ANNO 1827.

In 1826 Ingres and seven other artists received a commission to decorate the ceilings in the
Louvre extension built to house the Egyptian and Etruscan antiquities. Ingres saw the outline of
his composition immediately and began work in November. With the help of pupils the canvas was,
by December 1827, sufficiently complete to be fixed to the ceiling of the Salle Clarac, in time for
the opening of the Salon. The iconography of Homer's followers required careful documentation,
followed by intensive life-study, and, even allowing for Ingres's facility, it seems extraordinary that
the painting was presentable within the year. The composition comes mainly from Raphael's
Parnassus. The ancients are ranged mostly on the upper stage; the moderns are in the orchestra pits.
Homer, seated above personifications of the *Iliad* and the *Odyssey*, receives a wreath from a winged
Victory. The choice of the forty-two followers of Homer, as D. Ternois indicates, is conventionally
classic with occasionally a more personal note. Shakespeare and Mozart are included, while
Raphael, elevated with Michelangelo to the ranks of the ancients, is led by Apelles towards Homer.
Virgil, similarly, leads Dante. The idea of the great men of the ages paying tribute to Homer could
have been known to Ingres from contemporary literary images which probably derive from
Dante's visit to the limbo where the ancients were confined in *The Inferno*. The age of Ingres,
however, moved Aristotle from the centre of the vision—he is barely visible beside Michelangelo—
and put Homer in his place. The theme had personal significance for Ingres at a time when he was
making claims for membership of the classical tradition and saw his rôle in terms of its defence.
The ceiling was received politely, without enthusiasm. It makes no concession to Baroque
illusionism and was conceived as an upright easel picture fixed to the ceiling; but the composition
works extremely well in the box-like Salle Clarac, fringed with mock Pompeian decorations.

49 *Homer Deified*
PARIS, Musée du Louvre, Cabinet des Dessins. Black chalk, pen and ink wash on paper 21 × 31 cm.
Signed: J.-A.-D. Ingres inv. Pinxit Delineavit.

Ingres surprisingly once claimed that, unlike other artists, he never made repetitions of his own
works; he had in mind the fact that the numerous copies which he made of his pictures did not
simply repeat a successful pattern but attempted to improve upon the original. His constant
dissatisfaction made him a notoriously slow finisher and led him to rework, and often to spoil,
finished compositions. When, therefore, he was obliged to provide his engravers with reduced
drawings of his pictures, he could not resist the temptation to improve on his original scheme. The
drawing which he began for the engraver in 1840 of *The Apotheosis of Homer* (Plate 48) was not
finished until 1865 and included an extra thirty-six figures and a background frieze based on the
engravings of Flaxman. Alterations were made up to the last minute in the choice of spectators at
Homer's apotheosis. At first he intended to sacrifice Mozart to historical propriety but his passion
for the composer was too strong in the event. Other figures from the painting were omitted,
however, and the final choice of those included in the dynasty of Homer is altogether more orthodox
than the band of 1827 which included many personal favourites among the classics.

50 *Portrait of Charles X in Coronation Robes*
BAYONNE, Musée Bonnat. Oil on canvas 129 × 90 cm.
Signed: J. Ingres pxit 1829.

Charles X holds the same regalia as the Emperor
Napoleon in Ingres's portrait of 1806, but his grasp
seems timid by comparison. The portrait of Charles X
was not, in origin, a large public spectacle like the
portrait of the emperor. Ingres was invited to attend the
coronation at Rheims in 1825 to prepare drawings for
illustrations of the event for engraving. The present
portrait, commissioned by the comte de Fresne, closely
follows the scheme of one engraving. The background
was added, however, and the king's hand raised higher
than in the drawing to give more nobility to the gesture.
But the portrait remains essentially a miniature, trans-
posed from its original setting without complete success.

(opposite)
51 *Portrait of Monsieur Bertin*
PARIS, Musée du Louvre. Oil on canvas 116 × 96 cm. Signed: Ingres Pinxit, 1832.

Louis-François Bertin founded the *Journal des Débats* after the collapse of the Directoire on 18
Brumaire [1799] to reflect his own interests and beliefs, a political philosophy of sober liberalism
with a large corner reserved for the arts. Ingres's portrait is universally known as '*Monsieur Bertin*',
as though the absence of a fixed rank defines a quality of intimacy lacking in the more elegant and
official male images, such as those of Gouriev (Plate 44) and Pastoret (Plate 45). Indeed, Ingres's
first thoughts for Bertin were in the more austere mould of the Gouriev and Pastoret portraits and
of the second portrait of Bartolini (Plate 42), but, sensing the incongruity of the pose, he could not
make progress and wept with despair during sessions of fruitless work. Ingres found the final pose
when he caught sight of Bertin sitting in conversation with a friend (accounts differ as to details),
and, once found, the image was realized in the month. The result is an intimate and direct account
of Bertin's strong but kindly personality, which makes none of the concessions to charm common in
this type of portraiture. The colours are drab and unrelieved by the bright notes which Ingres
usually put into his male portraits. Bertin's chair, a sole and essential accessory in this seated
portrait, was made an integral part of the composition, anchoring the pyramidal form at one
corner. Its heavy polished back defines the solid mass of Bertin with its broad curve, while the
dark, plain mahogany matches the predominance of wooden colours in the picture. The portrait was
well received at the Salon of 1833, but Bertin's daughter was disappointed with the effect: 'My
father had the appearance of a noble man; Ingres has made him into a stout farmer.'

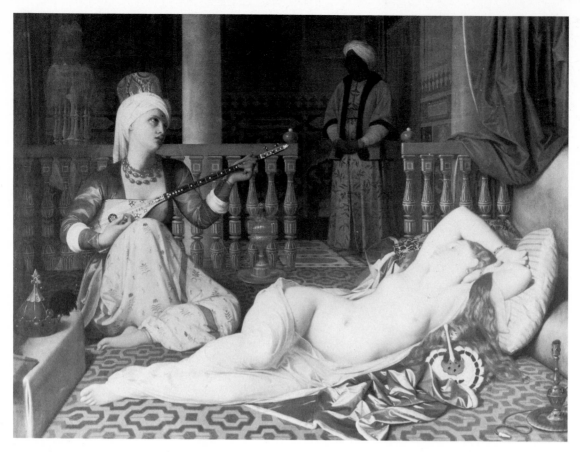

52 *The Odalisque with the Slave*
CAMBRIDGE (MASSACHUSETTS), Fogg Art Museum (Grenville L. Winthrop bequest). Oil on canvas
72 × 100 cm. Signed: J. Ingres Rom 1839.

In 1830, Ingres made a vain overture to recover his *Sleeping Woman* which he had last seen in
1814. He returned to the theme of the reposing nude in *The Odalisque with the Slave*, begun for
Marcotte in 1837 and finished in 1840. At first Ingres thought of including several other figures
besides the nude in order to enhance the composition but finally limited his composition to three
figures. The work was apparently done largely from studies already in his portfolio, presumably for
The Sleeping Woman, whose pose is repeated by the odalisque. Ingres had reservations about the
resulting loss of naturalism, but his patron seemed pleased. The artist, as always, researched his
work with care, possibly consulting Persian miniatures and exotic bric-a-brac. He specified a frame
'as baroque as possible (since it is Turkish) that is to say, everything you can find in the way of
ornaments which approximate to this country's style if possible' suitable for a work which was
'gracious and a little strange'. The strangeness is in the accessories; the gracious element derives
from Ingres's early fascination with the mannerisms of Girodet (fig. 6). This return in middle age
to studies dating from his youth provided a certain counterbalance to the growing realism of his
style.

(opposite)
VII *Portrait of Madame Moitessier*
WASHINGTON, National Gallery of Art (Samuel H. Kress collection). Oil on canvas 146·7 × 100·3
cm. Signed: J. A. D. Ingres Pxit ANº 1851.

Ingres at first declined the commission to paint Mme. Moitessier, as he had turned down Mme. de
Rothschild's initial overture, even at the request of Marcotte, who had been her father's junior
colleague in the administration of forests. Eventually, however, Ingres succumbed to her charms,
and thought of painting her on a canapé with her daughter at her knees, an intimate Davidian
motif which he had used in a number of his portrait drawings. As with the early versions of the
portraits of Mme. de Rothschild and Mme. d'Haussonville, this was a false start, and Ingres chose
instead a stately, upright pose, very formal, without any suggestion of a smile. The contrast
between the black of lace and velvet and the damask of the wall, framing the sitter's head and
shoulders, is broken up by the lively touches in the pink roses in her hair, her jewellery and yellow
gloves. The dress was painted in a few sittings in 1851; in June Ingres painted in the hands and
arms and, finally, the head and shoulders. In October he added the jewels. Ingres originally
intended Mme. Moitessier to wear a short necklace and an elaborate Renaissance brooch, but,
again, changed his mind at the last minute in favour of a simple cameo and a long string of
pearls. At the same time, perhaps thinking of the wreathed head in a mural at Naples which
inspired his next portrait of Mme. Moitessier, he abandoned his intention to give her an elaborate
hairstyle. She appears to be about to leave for the evening; her handkerchief, gloves and fur, 'a sort
of evening wrap, the sort you wear when you go out to a ball' as Ingres requested, lie on the chair.

53 *The Martyrdom of St. Symphorien*

AUTUN, Cathedral of Saint-Lazare. Oil on canvas 407 × 339 cm. Signed: J. A. Ingres, 1834.

In 1824 the comte de Vichy, bishop of Autun, wrote to the Minister of the Interior requesting a picture to replace a *Holy Family* removed to Paris during the Revolution. The minister gave the commission to Ingres, who visited Autun in November 1826 to inspect the site of the saint's martyrdom. His work for the Louvre on *The Apotheosis of Homer* prevented him from making progress until 1828, and the painting was not finished until 1834, nearly ten years after the original commission. If the wording of the commission for *The Vow of Louis XIII* had been brief and open to various interpretations, the bishop's programme was, by contrast, long and detailed and left little to the artist's imagination. The commission laid down Ingres's source for the Roman gate in the background (Laborde's *Monuments de la France*) and insisted that the costumes had to be Roman from the reign of the Antonines. Ingres documented the work with care, making wooden models for the helmets, breastplates, fasces and standards. He did not, however, entirely overcome the complexities of the subject, for the relationship between the figures of Symphorien and his mother, making a square shape on the surface of the canvas, destroys the sense of perspective. Ingres claimed to have painted the work while 'digesting Michelangelo'. The muscles of the lictors and soldiers show a general debt to the Sistine Chapel, which may also have been responsible for the flattened perspective. The mother clasping her child on the left is close to a detail from *The Deluge* on the Sistine ceiling. The poor reception given to *St. Symphorien* at the Salon of 1834 resolved Ingres to avoid future Salons and, although offers were not lacking, the episode, with a few exceptions, ended his career as a painter of important state commissions.

(opposite)

VIII *Portrait of Madame Moitessier*

LONDON, National Gallery. Oil on canvas 120 × 92 cm. Signed: J. Ingres 1856 AET LXXVI.

In the period of renewed energy in the early 1850s Ingres had scarcely finished the portrait of Mme. Moitessier now in Washington (Plate VII), before he turned again to the abandoned seated version begun in 1844. The second attempt gave him the same difficulties as the first. Ingres at one time had favoured a yellow dress but, at the last moment, chose the white printed silk with an intricate brooch, similar to the one which he rejected for the three-quarter length 1851 portrait. The blue fan, propped against the wall, with its motif of peacock feathers, and the oriental vase add a note of the exotic to the modern odalisque lounging on the damask sofa. Her pose, dating from 1844, recalls the reclining convention which Ingres used in a number of earlier portraits, but it was combined with a pose from a mural from Herculaneum, which gives her pagan grandeur. The mirror endows the painting with depth and contrast to the head, compensating for the rich and otherwise distracting wealth of detail. The leg of the gilt console and the reflections in the glass show that the canvas was placed at an angle to the mirror in order to separate the model's head from her reflection, but the rigid geometry of the composition and a slight fault in perspective conflict with the illusion of recession.

54 *Portrait of the Comte Louis-Mathieu Molé*

PARIS, collection of the Noailles family. Oil on canvas 147 × 114 cm. Signed: J. Ingres Pinxit 1834.

The idea of this composition evolved from discarded studies for the portrait of Bertin (Plate 51).
The spare, simple pose of Louis Philippe's prime minister, leaning on an antique chair of turned
wood before the fireplace in an otherwise fairly empty space typifies the official portrait style which
Ingres initiated in the portrait of Gouriev (Plate 44). A quill pen, the politician's attribute, lies on
the mantelpiece. Ingres began the portrait in 1833 and completed it before he left for Italy the
following year.

(opposite left)

55 *Portrait of Ferdinand-Philippe, duc d'Orléans*

VERSAILLES, Musée Historique. Oil on canvas 218 × 132 cm. Signed: J. Ingres pxit 1844.

The duc d'Orléans, eldest son of King Louis Philippe, wrote personally to Ingres in 1840 to secure
his portrait by the artist, a request Ingres could not refuse. Painting began in November 1841, and
it was finished by the following April. The formula for the portrait was familiar to Ingres, a tall,

lean figure with minimal accessories set within an ample space which serves to keep the model at a distance. His eyes look down on the spectator, and he holds a single glove in his left hand. Ingres had only to hesitate over the position of the hat and hands. The red of the duc's trousers, of which there is a dull reflection in the colour of the wall and curtain, gives the same dominant note as the lining of Gouriev's cloak, adding strength to the dark costume. Ingres insisted that the duc's military dress should be without any embroidery but could not persuade him to put cloth buttons on his jacket in place of the metal ones already there. The spare, uncluttered elegance of the portrait set new standards for nineteenth-century official portraits, but Ingres resented the time spent on portraits, and there are no major male portraits from the remaining twenty years of his life. Following the duc's death in an accident with his horses two months after the completion of the portrait, Ingres was involved in painting and supervising copies, of which the total has been reckoned at nineteen. The commission of this copy for the Musée Historique at Versailles specified a full length which destroyed Ingres's favourite balance between the elongated three-quarter length and the squarish canvas of the first version, now in the collection of the comte de Paris.

(*above right*)
56 *St. Ferdinand, King of Castile and León*
PARIS, Musée du Louvre. Oil on canvas 210 × 92 cm. Signed: J. Ingres fecit 1842.

On 13 July 1842 the duc d'Orléans, heir to the French throne, was killed in a fall from his carriage near Neuilly, outside Paris. King Louis Philippe decided at once to build a chapel on the spot where his son had died. On 26 July the king proposed that Ingres alone should design the stained glass for the chapel on account of the late duc's affection for the artist. Ingres completed the whole series of seventeen cartoons in less than two months. The chapel, rebuilt in 1971 at the Porte des Ternes, was inaugurated on the anniversary of the duc's death in July 1843. Ingres gave the patron saints of several members of the Orléans family the features of their protégés; the face of St. Ferdinand, King of Castile, is that of Ferdinand-Philippe, duc d'Orléans. Like all the other fourteen saints in the series, St. Ferdinand stands inside a rich frame combining Gothic and Byzantine elements which pick up the circular movement of the orb and halo, yet there was no attempt to produce a pastiche of medieval glass painting. Ingres's native elegance of drawing and strong sense of colour were brilliantly employed in the medium when the craftsmen of Sèvres transferred his designs to the chapel windows.

57 *Luigi Cherubini and the Muse of Lyric Poetry*
PARIS, Musée du Louvre. Oil on canvas 105 × 94 cm. Signed: J. Ingres Pinx. Paris 1842; inscribed:
L. CHERUBINI COMPR. NE A FLOR. 1760. Me DE L'INST. Dr DU CONSERVATOIRE.

Ingres's portrait of Cherubini, painted in 1833 and largely re-worked in 1842, was the only portrait
he painted of his many musical friends. At first, he painted a simple intimate study of the
composer leaning on a table, but later, after he had gone to Rome in 1834, he thought of making a
more important public image of Cherubini, perhaps identifying with his colleague at the Institut as
a champion of orthodoxy. When he returned from Rome in 1841, Ingres retrieved the portrait
from Cherubini and drastically altered this original to its present appearance. We can reconstruct
the first version with the aid of existing studies and a copy, now in Cincinnati, which Ingres
painted in Rome, presumably from the studies as the original was still in Paris. Where this copy
departed from the original, in the position of the hands and in the accessories, the work was
entrusted to Ingres's pupil, Henri Lehmann. Assuming that the Cincinnati copy more or less
corresponds to the original appearance of the Louvre portrait, Ingres must have cut the head out
of the first version and pasted it on to a much larger canvas; the outlines of this inset are clearly
visible in the Louvre picture. This allowed Ingres to show Cherubini resting his elbow not on a
common table but on the plinth of a classical pilaster and also gave room for the insertion of a
Muse of Lyric Poetry, standing over her protégé like the allegorical figure in the Homer ceiling
(Plate 48). The poor state of the additions, caused by extensive use of bitumen, which Ingres never
used, and the weakness of the drawing of the foreshortened arm, which Ingres himself admitted,
indicate the work of a pupil. Following the precedent of David's exhibition of 1799, Ingres held a

paying exhibition of the portrait in his studio in 1842, which, unlike most enterprises of this sort in nineteenth-century Paris, was a popular success. Cherubini died on 15 March of the same year and on 18 June King Louis Philippe bought the portrait for 8000 francs. For many years it was the only portrait admitted to the gallery of modern art in the Luxembourg Palace, a tribute to Ingres's attempt from this time on to give the humble portrait genre the cachet of history painting.

(*above*)
58 *Portrait of Madame Reiset*
CAMBRIDGE (MASSACHUSETTS), Fogg Art Museum (Grenville L. Winthrop bequest). Oil on canvas 60 × 47 cm. approximately. Signed: J. Ingres Pinxit Enghien 1846.

In 1835 Frédéric Reiset, later curator of the drawings in the Louvre and Direceur des Beaux-Arts during the Third Republic, arrived in Italy on holiday after his marriage to his cousin, Hortense Reiset. The couple met Ingres at the Ecole de Rome and became his lifelong friends. The artist and his wife were frequent guests at the Reisets' chalet on Lake Enghien, where this portrait of Hortense was painted in 1846. The unusually small format of the portrait is no doubt explained by the fact that it was not painted in Ingres's studio.

59 *Portrait of the princesse de Broglie*
NEW YORK, Metropolitan Museum of Art (Robert Lehman collection). Oil on canvas 106×88 cm.
Signed: J. Ingres Pit 1853.

After the disasters and hesitations of the 1840s, the early 1850s were for Ingres a time of
achievement. The portrait of Mme. Moitessier (Plate VII), begun again in 1851, was finished within
the year and the portrait of Mme. Gonse, long abandoned, was taken up in 1851 and finished in
1852. Ingres began painting the portrait of the princesse de Broglie, sister-in-law of the vicomtesse
d'Haussonville (Plate VI), in 1851 'to the content of everyone and without difficulty' and, although
work was interrupted in 1852 by trouble with his eyes, he had finished the portrait by the end of
June 1853. The casual pose of the princesse de Broglie leaning on the back of an arm chair derives
from the first portrait of the vicomtesse d'Haussonville, but the shawl, fan and gloves waiting on the
chair suggest that, like Mme. Moitessier, she is on the point of leaving for the evening.

61 *Antiochus and Stratonice*
CHANTILLY, Musée Condé. Oil on canvas 57 × 98 cm. Signed: J. Ingres F^{at} Rome, 1840.

The story of Antiochus's passion for his step-mother, told by Plutarch, was a commonplace in the art and theatre of Ingres's youth. The outline of Ingres's composition derives from a painting by Girodet illustrating the moment traditionally singled out by artists when the doctor diagnoses Antiochus's illness by the racing of his pulse in the presence of Stratonice. Ingres began a work on this theme in 1807 while hesitating over a choice of subjects to send to the Paris Académie. This work was not finished and is now only known from a preparatory drawing of 1807 (Plate 10) which is closer to Girodet than the painting of 1840, commissioned by the duc d'Orléans as a pendant to Delaroche's *Assassination of the duc de Guise*. The contrast between the early drawing and the Orléans picture highlights the influence of Ingres's experience of historic genre painting during the Restoration, not only in the realism of the setting, which was painstakingly researched, but also in the small scale which was determined by Delaroche's painting. The decorative, frieze-like effect of the drawing was sacrificed in the painting to a three-dimensional appearance. Ingres spent six years working on the picture, experimenting with poses—Antiochus's gesture as he tries to shield his sight from the fatal view of Stratonice was studied fifty-five times—and documenting the local colour with the help of Baltard, the architect of les Halles. Stratonice's pose was taken from an Antique type. The outstanding success of the picture when it was exhibited privately in the Palais Royal in 1840 prepared the way for Ingres's triumphant return to Paris in 1841.

(*page* 79)
60 *Portrait of the Baronne James de Rothschild*
PARIS, private collection. Oil on canvas 141·8 × 101·5 cm. Signed: J. Ingres Pinxit 1848; inscribed: B^{ne} BETTY DE ROTHSCHILD.

On his return from Rome, Ingres turned down a request from the baronne de Rothschild to paint her portrait. The baronne insisted with personal calls and gifts of game, and after two years Ingres relented. By February 1843 he had finished the head, but by June 1844, sensing that he had made a false start, he decided to begin again. Progress was delayed by the work for Dampierre and other portraits on hand at the same time. By June 1847, the improved version was nearly finished; 'cursed portraits', he remarked, 'they constantly prevent me from striding forward to great things which I cannot get on with, a portrait is such a hard thing.' The pose of Mme. de Rothschild, set unusually low in the picture frame, allows her astonishing pink satin dress to spread out and fill the bottom of the picture frame. 'Her eyes gleam with the wit on the tip of her tongue' wrote Gautier. 'This is a sparkling conversation, begun in a ballroom or over the dinner table, which continues afterwards.'

62 *The Age of Gold*

CAMBRIDGE (MASSACHUSETTS), Fogg Art Museum (Grenville L. Winthrop bequest). Oil on canvas
48×62 cm. Signed: J. Ingres Pin^t MDCCCLXII Aetatis LXXXII.

In 1839 the duc de Luynes offered Ingres a generous commission for two murals to decorate his
recently renovated château at Dampierre. Ingres was offered 70,000 francs for the two works and
apparent freedom in all the details. Ingres hesitated, at first, between oil and fresco and eventually
compromised by choosing oil applied directly on to the wall, which meant that all painting had to
be done in the château although the many life-studies were drawn entirely in Paris. Delayed by
royal commissions, Ingres did not begin work in the château until 1843, but by 1845, with the help
of pupils, work on one panel, *The Age of Gold*, was well advanced and the companion, *The Age of
Iron*, was in hand. Dr. Schlenoff has suggested that the theme of the Golden Age had Miltonic
overtones for Ingres. Certainly, thoughts of Paradise were never far from the minds of nineteenth-
century idealists. Ingres was convinced that his own times were an Age of Iron. Conscious that he
was not following the Renaissance account of the Golden Age as a time of pastoral orgy, Ingres
thought that he was restoring Hesiod's Antique vision. Astraea, on the left, teaches justice, while
Saturn, balancing her on the left of the Dampierre mural but in the background of this reduced
variant in Cambridge, watches over a crowd of families and lovers in the centre. Ingres followed
Flaxman's mistake, however, of illustrating the Golden Age, which Hesiod dated from a period
before the division of the sexes, in terms of the ideal family. The general motif was derived from
Watteau and included elements of Mantegna's *Parnassus* in the Louvre. Several figures, as Dr. Naef
has discovered, were taken from contemporary Italian prints of a Flaxmanesque character. The
parents embracing in the foreground right recall the poses of *Raphael and the Fornarina* (Plate 33),
inspired by the *Madonna della Sedia*, an appropriate and no doubt conscious reference in this
nostalgic vision of a lost Utopia to Ingres's invariable ideal. Following the death of his wife in
1849, Ingres refused to continue work on the panels, leaving *The Age of Gold* unfinished and *The
Age of Iron* a bare, architectural background. Apart from the position of Saturn and a few less
important alterations in other figures, this reduced variant, painted by Ingres in 1862, is
essentially similar to the unfinished mural still visible at Dampierre.

63 *The Birth of Venus*

CHANTILLY, Musée Condé. Oil on canvas 163 × 92 cm. approximately. Signed: J. Ingres Faciebat 1808 et 1848.

Ingres owned a stock of unfinished canvases and studies dating from his first years in Rome when he was hesitating over a choice of subjects to submit to the Académie in Paris. Choice was restricted to Antique myth and history by the academic nature of the work. In 1807–08 he began work on *The Birth of Venus*. At first Ingres thought of the modest pose of *The Medicean Venus* but altered this to the image used by Apelles in Antiquity, showing the goddess tiring her hair as she rides to the shore on the foam. The winged *amorini*, added to turn an academic study into a composition, gained prominence as the work continued. Ingres abandoned the painting, however, until 1821 when he received a commission from J. L. Leblanc, his patron in Florence, to finish the sketch. He was working on the picture in December 1822 but eventually the subject was abandoned again, until he received a commission in 1847 to complete it. Ingres worked on *The Birth of Venus*, with Parnassian indifference, through the 1848 revolution, signing the work in June and putting it on show in his studio. His pupil, Amaury-Duval, was disappointed with the finished effect. The pale sky of the first version had turned dark blue, and the charm of the sketchy touch was lost. Between 1808 and 1848 Ingres had subdued the expressive mannerism of his early style.

(opposite)
64 *The Source*

PARIS, Musée du Louvre. Oil on canvas 163 × 80 cm. Signed: J. Ingres, 1856.

According to Amaury-Duval, *The Source* was originally a realistic life-study, begun in Florence in the 1820s and identical in pose to *The Birth of Venus* (Plate 63). Like the *Venus*, for which this painting was possibly a life-study executed when Ingres was working on the earlier picture for Leblanc, *The Source* remained unfinished in the artist's studio for over thirty years. Perhaps encouraged by the success of the *Venus*, Ingres returned to the figure in 1855, adding the urn and background with extensive help from his pupils, Paul Balze and Alexandre Desgoffe. The transformation into an allegorical figure of a spring was probably inspired by Goujon's sixteenth-century figures on the Fountain of the Innocents in Paris which Ingres had copied. The success of *The Source* was overwhelming. Ingres nerved himself to ask for 25,000 francs when he sold it to the Comte Duchâtel; 'not much' he added 'for all the fuss that is made of it in Paris'. Many contemporary artists looked to it for a model in their search for 'style', and most of Ingres's early biographers, Lapauze included, classed it with his finest work. Recent opinion tends to agree with Amaury-Duval that the added paint is dull and the pose insipid. The faults are in the execution; the head does not convincingly connect with the body, but the torso is painted with familiar subtlety.

83

65 *The Virgin with the Host*

PARIS, Musée du Louvre. Oil on canvas 133 cm. diameter. Signed: J. Ingres Pit, 1854.

Ingres's Madonnas derived largely from his studies for *The Vow of Louis XIII* (Plate 47). The first in this series was commissioned from Ingres by the future Tsar Alexander II in 1839. Ingres, angered by his brief official letter of thanks when the work was delivered, suggested to the engraver that when he reproduced the work, he should remove the tsarevitch's patron saints and substitute two angels with candlesticks and incense. This idea was retained for the Louvre picture, commissioned by the Minister of the Interior in the 1840s but not delivered on account of the fall of the Orléans monarchy. Ingres offered to finish the painting for the state in 1851 in answer to an official commission. This suggestion was accepted, and the work delivered in 1854. The accessories were derived from *The Virgin with the Candlesticks* from the studio of Raphael. The heavy symmetry in the faces of Ingres's Madonnas, unlike the more lively type of Raphael's Virgins, can be associated with a passage in Ingres's notes. 'Portrait of the Virgin Mary. Here, says Nicephore Callistus, collecting the tradition, is what can be discovered about her. She had arched, black eyebrows, a long nose and red lips . . . her face, shaped like an olive, neither round nor pointed but slightly elongated, was the colour of cheese; unsmiling, as though untroubled, she spoke little. . . .'

(opposite)

66 *Joan of Arc at the Coronation of Charles VII*

PARIS, Musée du Louvre. Oil on canvas 240 × 178 cm. Signed: J. Ingres Pit, 1854.

Ingres probably had his portrait of Charles X (Plate 50) in mind when he composed this picture of St. Joan at the coronation of Charles VII which, like all coronations of French kings, took place at

Rheims. Both paintings derived from drawings made to be engraved. The original drawing of St. Joan, published in *Le Plutarque français* in 1844, works effectively, like the portrait of Charles X, as a romantic vignette, but was not suited for the embellishments which Ingres imposed when transforming it into a painting. In the engraving Joan's left arm has a pretty angularity, like Charles X's arm in the early version of his portrait. Ingres ennobled this gesture in the painting by imitating the changes made to the king's arm in the final portrait. The painting of *Joan of Arc* was already in hand when Ingres received an offer in 1851 to paint a work of his own choice for the state. Ingres's offer of this picture and the half-finished *Virgin with the Host* (Plate 65) was accepted, and the works were delivered in 1854. Ingres originally intended to paint a single figure, again like *Charles X*, but, always conscious of the need to add importance to a composition, he inserted five other figures, including a portrait of himself as Joan's squire. The addition increased the price of the picture from 10,000 to 15,000 francs. Much of the actual paintwork was done by Ingres's pupil, Raymond Balze, which no doubt accounts for a flatness in the execution.

67 *The Apotheosis of Napoleon*
PARIS, Musée Carnavalet. Oil on canvas 48 cm. diameter. Unsigned.

Ingres hesitated before accepting the commission to decorate a ceiling for the Salon of the Emperor in the restored Hôtel de Ville in Paris, although he had suggested such an enterprise to the prefecture of the Seine in 1840. His abortive work at the Château de Dampierre and the fall of the Orléans monarchy had unnerved his confidence in being able to finish his commissions. *The Apotheosis of Napoleon*, commissioned on 2 March 1853, had to be completed by the end of the year, and eventually Ingres accepted, submitted a proposal which was approved and finished the work on time. As it was destroyed in the fire of 1871 it is difficult to judge the effect of this scheme from the preliminary sketch in the Carnavalet. Surrounded by the voussures with emblematic figures of the capitals captured by Napoleon, like the seven towns disputing Homer's birth along one side of the Homer ceiling in the Louvre, the effect must have been impressive. The sketch shows Ingres hesitating between a circle and a square, perhaps altering an originally square idea, as in *Ossian* and *The Turkish Bath*, to correspond with a circular movement in the main group. The lower figures would adequately square off the central movement but lose their *raison d'être* inside a circle. The idealization recalls the early *Venus Wounded by Diomedes* (Plate 4), and the sources were similar, Flaxman and the Antique. Girodet had lost prominence, but there is an echo of Prudhon's *Divine Vengeance* in the figure of Nemesis pursuing Crime and Anarchy. The sketch shows Ingres's tendency to sacrifice the mannerism of his early work for the sake of naturalism. When asked what model he used for the horses he answered 'Phidias and the horses of an omnibus'. The commission brought him into contact with the Imperial family, whose patronage partly compensated for the loss of that of the Orléans family.

69 *The Rape of Europa*
CAMBRIDGE (MASSACHUSETTS), Fogg Art Museum (Grenville L. Winthrop bequest). Watercolour on paper 30·1 × 42·5 cm. Signed: J. Ingres E^it. sur un trait de Vase Grec. 1863.

In the mid-eighteenth century almost the only source available to an artist who wished to study the Antique was a heterogeneous collection of marbles. The growing awareness at the end of the century that the so called 'Etruscan' red figured earthenware represented purest Greek art gave painters access to a new range of motifs for treating Antique themes. Although Ingres collected Greek pottery, noting its usefulness in this respect, the main influence of vase painting on his style was indirectly transmitted through Girodet and Flaxman. This watercolour, copied from an engraving published in 1846 after a vase in the British Museum, was, as an inscription added by Ingres explains, an attempted reconstruction of a lost Greek painting preserved, according to Ingres's ingenious theory, in a copy on the vase which explains the addition of modelling and colour to the characteristic outline style of the vase painter. The unusual stylization is explained by Ingres's adherence to western Europe's preoccupation with the lost art of Greece. Like Botticelli, Ingres was attracted by the themes associated with lost Antique paintings like *Calumny* and *The Birth of Venus*. *The Rape of Europa* is an erudite side current of this passionate involvement with the art of the ancient world.

(*opposite*)
68 *The Birth of the Muses*
PARIS, Musée du Louvre. Watercolour on paper mounted on copper 25·7 × 53·2 cm. Signed: Ingres 1856.

In the early 1850s Ingres, like a number of his fellow artists, reacted to the appearance of a new Napoleon by drawing on his stock of classical allusion. In fact, state patronage under Napoleon III did not give much scope for illustrating the virtues of Antiquity, although the emperor's republican cousin, Prince Napoleon-Joseph, amply compensated for this official neglect. He lived in a mock Pompeian villa in the centre of Paris, with rooms in Turkish and Pompeian taste reflecting the fusion of Antiquity and the orient prevalent in the mid-century imagination. The prince owned *The Turkish Bath*, had his portrait painted as an Antique medallion by Ingres and commissioned *The Birth of the Muses* from the artist for insertion into a model temple designed by the architect Hittorf as a present for the actress Rachel. Ingres began work on the watercolour in Paris in May 1856 and finished it at his country retreat by August. The temple was dedicated appropriately to the dramatic Muse, but Ingres represented the birth of the last Muse, Erato, in the presence of Jupiter, in order to include all the Muses in his picture. The composition made use of a number of classical motifs, the Elgin marbles, the Jupiter of Olympus and the statue in the Vatican which had inspired Stratonice's reflective pose.

70 *The Turkish Bath*

PARIS, Musée du Louvre. Oil on canvas pasted on wood 108 cm. diameter. Signed: J. Ingres Pinx^t. MDCCCLXII Aetatis LXXXII.

Ingres reused *The Valpinçon Bather* (Plate 18) in 1828 as the centre of a small scene set in a Turkish bath, a painting now, also, in the Louvre. In the early 1850s, Ingres returned to this idea, amalgamating *The Valpinçon Bather* with the pose of the musician in *The Odalisque with the Slave* (Plate 52) and adding some two dozen other nude bathers derived from prints in picturesque travel books. The episode follows an account of a visit to a harem in Adrianopolis from Lady Mary Wortley Montagu's *Letters*, published in translation in Paris in 1805. Apart from the eroticism of the theme, Ingres, as Schlenoff points out, was intrigued by Lady Mary's comparison between the baths in Turkey and those of ancient Greece. *The Valpinçon Bather* slips easily between Antiquity and the orient in Ingres's work, and perhaps the artist was inspired to take up the theme again by the successful exhibition at the Salon of 1852 of *The Tepidarium*, a scene set in a Pompeian bath house by his pupil Chassériau. Ingres's picture, which seems to have been at first intended for Count Demidov, was finished in 1859 and sold to the count's brother-in-law, Prince Napoleon-Joseph Bonaparte. At the request of his wife, upset by the excessive nudity, the prince exchanged *The Turkish Bath* for Ingres's self-portrait of 1804. The picture, having already been once enlarged, was then transformed by Ingres from its original square shape into a tondo, making alterations necessary round the edge of the composition. These were not finished until 1863.